GREAT LIVES OBSERVED

Gerald Emanuel Stearn, *General Editor*

EACH VOLUME IN THE SERIES VIEWS THE CHARACTER AND
ACHIEVEMENT OF A GREAT WORLD FIGURE IN THREE PERSPEC-
TIVES—THROUGH HIS OWN WORDS, THROUGH THE OPINIONS
OF HIS CONTEMPORARIES, AND THROUGH RETROSPECTIVE JUDG-
MENTS—THUS COMBINING THE INTIMACY OF AUTOBIOGRA-
PHY, THE IMMEDIACY OF EYEWITNESS OBSERVATION, AND
THE OBJECTIVITY OF MODERN SCHOLARSHIP.

GERALD EMANUEL STEARN *studied at the University of Illinois,
the London School of Economics and Political Science, and
Columbia University, where he taught American and Compar-
ative History. He edited the critical symposium* McLuhan: Hot
& Cool *and conceived the* Great Lives Observed *series, of
which he is general editor.*

GREAT LIVES OBSERVED

GOMPERS

Edited by
GERALD EMANUEL STEARN

*It is not a pleasant task
to destroy men's dreams.*

—F. LAURRELL TO GOMPERS, 1873

A SPECTRUM BOOK

PRENTICE-HALL, INC., ENGLEWOOD CLIFFS, N. J.

Grateful acknowledgment is made to the following libraries for research assistance: AFL-CIO (Washington), Columbia University, Wisconsin State Historical Society, New York Public Library, and Catholic University. Lenworth A. Gunther provided indispensable help in assembling materials.

Current printing (last number):
10 9 8 7 6 5 4 3 2 1

PRENTICE-HALL INTERNATIONAL, INC. (*London*)

PRENTICE-HALL OF AUSTRALIA, PTY. LTD. (*Sydney*)

PRENTICE-HALL OF CANADA, LTD. (*Toronto*)

PRENTICE-HALL OF INDIA PRIVATE LIMITED (*New Delhi*)

PRENTICE-HALL OF JAPAN, INC. (*Tokyo*)

This book, and the Great Lives Observed series,
are dedicated to my mother
Riva Stearn
and to the memory of my father
Samuel Stearn

Contents

vii

ix

Introduction

I think that you will realize that I am a rather well organized man . . ."

—SAMUEL GOMPERS (1911)

Samuel Gompers died without regret. "Say to [the workers]," he whispered as he lay dying, "that I kept the faith." The faith, according to Gompers, was a tenacious belief in the power of organized workers to achieve a better life during the brutal years of early American industrialism. He created and led the American Federation of Labor from the 1880s until his death in 1924. By the end of his life he had become a living monument dedicated to rigid principles and cautious enthusiasm. To many of his contemporaries, Gompers was "a labor statesman" in the power politics of modern economic relations. To others, he was a working-class traitor, an opportunist who freely gave to capitalists what lesser men would have sold.

Gompers was born in the slums of London in 1850, the son of Dutch-Jewish workers. He learned his father's cigarmaking craft after a brief adventure as a shoemaker's apprentice. By 1860, though only ten, Gompers became a full-time member of the working class, earning one shilling a week. Hard times and a growing family forced Gompers' father, Solomon, to emigrate to America, then a nation torn by civil war. The family arrived in New York in 1863 during that city's murderous anti-Negro draft riots and immediately continued the inherited craft of cigar-making, working and living in the same wretched slum apartment near the Bowery. Young Sam soon left his workbench at home and began shaping and rolling tobacco for a number of cigar manufacturers. "Life in the factory," he recalled decades later, "is one of my most pleasant memories. I had real joy in living. I took an aristocratic joy in work." However appealing factory life may have been, Gompers, along with a group of fellow workers, tried to gain shorter hours and higher pay. He agitated for improved conditions, went on strike, was blacklisted, locked out, and unemployed before he was twenty. "On labor matters," Gompers wrote of his early days, "my thought was wild."

New York in the 1870s was an island haven for international radicals. Men wanted for political crimes in Europe or those defeated in their native countries during factional squabbles—the common cold of nine-

1

teenth century agitators—drifted over to the relative freedom of America. The German philosopher Karl Marx, the greatest radical of them all and the shrewdest student of working-class discontent, never left Europe for the North American republic but the seductive force of his ideas sailed with many boat-loads of angry young men. Gompers studied Marx, even learning German to read the first volume of the epic *Das Capital.* "His writings were a terrific indictment of society," Gompers said, "couched in the terms in general usage in that chaotic period of the labor movement. Terms as Marx used them often had a very different meaning from what became fixed in later years."

Marx wanted to change the desperate conditions of industrial life he observed in the middle of the nineteenth century. He studied history and the writings of the classical economists, Adam Smith, Riccardo, and Malthus. All history, Marx said, was the history of class conflict, and the nature of conflict was determined by the mode of production—how goods were produced and sold. Modern industrialism presented a new form of class conflict, between the workers (or the proletariat) and the capitalists (or the bourgeoisie). This conflict was pitilessly fought, the capitalists extracting labor and therefore profits from workers who were victims of "wage slavery." Materialism was the sole force in history. And History determined that the present stage of development was the capitalist one, a world where materialism was wedded to science. Men had little choice in determining their earthly existence: they belonged to one class or another, the proletariat or the bourgeoisie, the rich or the poor. The middle classes were merely transition stages for people on their way up or down. The state acted as the official clerk for capitalist managers; laws were instituted merely to protect the rights of private property. Religion taught workers that a better life was coming not in this, but in the next, world. People were lulled into complacency and resignation by churchmen who preached the complementary virtues of obedience and poverty. Meanwhile, as capitalism developed, the few became richer and the ranks of the working class swelled. But the worker's life deteriorated. Instabilities of the market place created panics, recessions and depressions. Workers became unemployed and now, forced to live near factories in towns and cities, were cut off from the land and food. They faced periodic starvation. As capitalism reached its higher stages, these crises grew in intensity. Workers were pushed deeper and deeper into the pits of misery. Capitalists themselves became economic cannibals, absorbing business rivals and monopolizing the market place. But, Marx predicted, there was a new world coming.

Marx preached revolution. The Laws of History, discovered by him using "scientific principles" of investigation, showed that the dominant class must fall, paradoxically by creating the means of its own destruction. As the working classes grew increasingly desperate, they would rebel and seize what the capitalists had stolen from them: the value of their labor. Formed into a class dictatorship, the proletariat would "expropriate the expropriators," repossessing the factories they slaved in, the shops where they traded, the railroads they built, and the houses they rented. Now they would organize society and the means of production on a rational basis for the common good and not the privileged few, building socialism, the historically appointed successor to capitalism. Gradually, a utopian world would evolve out of socialism, the world of communism, where the guiding principle of life would be: from each according to his ability, to each according to his needs. Communism would be the best and final stage in history, a Garden of Eden without, alas, God, where men would cultivate perfection and live joyously amidst sublime economic bounty.

The gospel of Marxism came to Gompers as a second Revelation. He retained throughout his life this catechism of industrial liturgy while rejecting, eventually, the prophet, Marx, himself. Unlike the utopian Socialists of his day, Gompers accepted both industrialism and capitalism as historically "correct" phenomena. He rejected such panaceas of the age as free silver, the Single Tax, civil service reform and prohibition as unscientific, sentimental dreams of middle-class reformers. Until a better world came, he accepted the "cash nexus" of society: wages; and the *permanent* struggle between workers and bosses for money and freedom. Materialism was the driving force in life. Economic, not political, rights determined relative freedom. He was hostile to the state and law; the antitrust movement had no attraction for him since capitalists devoured one another according to History, not the whims of transient politicians. Finally, Gompers never challenged modernity or turned away from the harsh materialism of reality.

America in the 1870s, the formative years of Gompers' intellectual life, was a Marxian delight. A predominantly agricultural country before the Civil War, the United States soon became a continental machine shop. The output of manufactured goods doubled between 1870 and 1890. Twenty million pounds of copper were purchased in 1871, nearly 88 million pounds in 1882. Pig-iron production increased from 1.8 million tons in 1870 to 10.3 million in 1890. Textile mills used nearly 800,000 bales of cotton in 1870, 2.6 million in 1891. Petroleum products increased seven times in twenty years to an average of 22 million barrels by 1890. The Bell telephone was displayed in 1876; by the mid-nineties over 300,000 phones were operating. Railroads connected the Atlantic and Pacific coasts. By 1890 railroad mileage in America (166,703) amounted to nearly a third of the world's. A national economy was created, lighted by Edison's incandescent bulb, first produced by him in 1879. Within ten years he became involved in a multi-million-dollar business operating power stations and producing electrical fixtures. And these great wonders of industrial production were brought by clever, inventive, ruthless, and domineering entrepreneurs who were Marxian stereotypes of all that was "good and bad" in capitalism. "Our money built these mills," said a textile manufacturer in the 1870s during a labor dispute, "and we propose to secure whatever benefits may be derived from the business." A shoe manufacturer proclaimed that his "experience with laboring men for twenty-one years and more" had convinced him that nothing "saves men from debauchery and crime so much as labor—and that 'til one is tired and ready to return to the domestic joys and duties of home. The dram-shop and the saloon are all favorable to a reduction of the hours of labor." When the president of Western Union was asked about the low wages of his employees and his absolute power to dictate working conditions, he replied: "All employment, all forms of labor, are governed by the laws of supply and demand."

As a diagnostician, Marx was obviously a genius; but as a prophet he was not a success. The horrors of capitalism existed. When would socialism and communism come? What were the workers to do *now* in order to hasten the socialistic future? Very little, Marx said. History could not be rushed; "objective" factors must be met. Be patient, he advised.

Gompers lacked patience. He accepted the Marxian analysis and, for a time, the glowing prediction of industrial man's fate. But he soon came under the influence of two European expatriates, primitive Marxists themselves, and veterans of countless socialist debates—Carl Ferdinand Laurrell, a radical seaman, and Adolph Strasser, a brilliant cigar unionizer. They adopted Gompers as an intellectual son and advised him to "go to the [socialist] meetings, learn all they have to give, read all they publish, but don't join." Carefully they led him through the maze of Marxian options, discounting each as either impractical or naive. Finally, Strasser and Laurrell persuaded Gompers that the only realistic means of opposing capitalism was the organizing of workers with common interests and shared complaints into groups or "trade unions." United by the discipline of urgency, these unions would confront employers with lists of nonnegotiable demands—for shorter hours, greater pay, better working conditions, more security, and freedom from excessive supervision. If employers refused to grant relief, the union would call a strike, its members refusing to work. Still anxious for the coming of socialism and utopia, Gompers wanted improvement, however insubstantial, now. Strasser, Laurrell, and Gompers, unlike Marx, were full-time members of the working class and the atractiveness of immediacy offered by trade unions was self-evident.

But the idea of trade unions in America was not invented by Gompers and his associates. The first recorded strike in this country occurred in 1741 when New York bakers refused to make bread because of the low pay. Guilds of skilled craftsmen were organized in Philadelphia and Boston before and after the Revolution. Workingmen's parties appeared during the Jacksonian period, but their programs were more reformist and middle-class than job oriented. The English common law, used by American courts to protect the rights of property, held labor organizations to be illegal conspiracies. Lord Mansfield, speaking near the end of the eighteenth century, declared that "Every man may work at any price he pleases, but a combination not to work under certain prices is an indictable offense." In 1842, however, in the famous case of *Commonwealth* vs. *Hunt*, the Supreme Court absolved labor unions of this repressive charge. By executive order in 1840, President Van Buren established a ten-hour day for federal employees; in 1852 the first union to maintain a permanent existence, the Typographers', was founded. New England shoemakers won a strike in 1860, and in the same decade the National Labor Union (1866) was organized, led by William Sylvis who favored 1) collaboration with European workers and newly freed Negroes, and 2) the money policies of the Greenback party. "When a just monetary system has been established," Sylvis wrote, "there will no longer exist a necessity for trade unions."

The barbaric attitudes of business and the hostility of the law weakened unionization. In the 1870s and '80s, for example, there were nearly 60,000 members of a Pennsylvania miners' union; after an unsuccessful strike in 1875 against a wage cut, the union practically dissolved. A shoemakers' union called the Knights of St. Crispin lost its entire membership of 50,000 in less than a decade, 1870–78. Indeed, although the labor force doubled between 1870 and 1890, there was a mere 20 percent increase in union members during the same period, the number going from 300,000 to 370,000. The savage repression of the Molly McGuire killer gangs who conspired against a wage cut in the Pennsylvania coal fields was a prelude to the extraordinary upheavals in 1877 during a national railroad workers' strike. Trains and depots were seized; militia fired at strikers, who shot back; railroad cars were looted and burned. Armed businessmen patroled the streets of several cities. The national press called the strike un-American and suggested that unions be outlawed. Failed strikes and misdirected energies did more to frustrate organized labor than legal or business vigilantes. The structure of organized labor seemed unable to cope with either the complexities of the business cycle and industrialism or the everyday management of its own affairs.

The Noble and Holy Order of the Knights of Labor became active in the 1870s, hoping to restrain capitalism by forming a coalition of middle-class reformers, craft unions and the masses of semi- and unskilled workers. Its brave motto—"An injury to one is the concern of all"—was a statement of hope rather than intention, for the Knights during their brief existence were weak, if not in numbers, then in effective power. The Knights demanded secrecy so that members would not be blacklisted for agitation; it practiced a semi-Masonic ritual filled with mystical mumbo jumbo; and it looked to the destruction of the wage system and the establishment of the cooperative commonwealth. The Knights were never a class organization, including as they did farmers, small shopkeepers and even larger employers. Its Assemblies were organized on a "mixed" basis, that is, they included both skilled and unskilled workers. Craft organizations were either condemned or ignored by the Order as too narrow and selfish. By the end of the 1880s the Knights counted over 700,000 members and seemed the primary agency for modern labor reform.

Although he belonged to the Knights, Gompers became impatient with the confused leadership, the neglect of unionization, and the political ambitions of the Order. Using the cigarmakers' experience as a testing ground, Gompers (led by Strasser and Laurrell) challenged the Knights from within and began a program of separate development, planning to replace the Knights as the dominant labor organization of their time.

The "new unionism" of Gompers parodied the emerging corporate structure of big business, although its most immediate example was the British Trades Union Congress (TUC). Skilled workers were gathered by craft into geographic, or shop, locals. The locals in turn were strongly bound to a national union of the craft led by an elected, full-time and well-paid administration which exercised firm control over member locals. Strike funds, centrally controlled, were accumulated and work stoppages were called with national approval, not local initiative. Benefits were paid members and their families for sickness, loss of income during periods of unemployment, and at death. An equalization process was devised so that the more-monied locals transferred funds to less prosperous ones. Trade agreements—contracts—were negotiated and signed between unions and employers on a craft basis. Special "union labels" were placed on approved products while nonunion goods were boycotted. Regular journals, filled with economic, social, and political as well as unions news, were encouraged. Paid organizers were sent out to unionize workers by craft. Members with political, ideological, or reformist tendencies were tolerated though not encouraged. Finally, a high and compulsory per capita tax was assessed to finance the operation. "Trade unions," Gompers once remarked, "are the business organizations of the workers."

The development of this "new unionism" affected the history of labor, both organized and unorganized, skilled and unskilled, for fifty years, from the 1880s until the Great Depression and the coming of the New Deal. By concentrating on economic matters, it broke with the reformist traditions of the Knights and its national predecessors; by stressing craft over semi- or unskilled workers, it broke apart the idealized working-class united front against employers. The main goals of this type of unionism were survival during bad economic times and effectiveness during prosperity—the substitution of craft, for class, consciousness. This was the "pure and simple" method: "pure" because it excluded nonunion workers; "simple" because it excluded theoretical agitation in favor of an insatiable materialism.

The scheme did well for fifty years because of the extraordinary talents of Gompers. Unlike Strasser or Laurrell, he spoke, read, and wrote English as his mother tongue. Unlike other immigrant labor leaders, his religious commitments (to Judaism) were slight. His early life in New York brought him in contact with most of the socialist activists of the period and his early study of Marx made him a formidable adversary of the Left as it repeatedly challenged the pure and simple philosophy. Gompers had a limitless reserve of energy, a brilliant public-speaking style, a gross but lucid literary technique, and he combined these talents with an ego born to be inflated. He knew how to run an office, handle correspondence, keep to a schedule, and organize mass meetings of union members. A shrewd parliamentarian, he learned to manage conventions as if they were stockholders' meetings, only he held most of the proxies. He was a superb tactician who knew how to turn his few moments of vulnerability into impervious façades. His humor was quick, aggressive, and when used against enemies, filled with the most corrosive epithets of the time. Scrupulously honest in financial affairs, he was a model of fiscal probity, unlike the politicians and businessmen he confronted. He lacked political or ideological ambitions. His memory was encyclopedic, and his rhetoric, if tiresome, had the strength of familiarity to his varied audiences. He loved men, he said in his autobiography; he liked being with them, talking and drinking with them. But most importantly, he had a passion for organization.

The 1880s saw a return to prosperity following the panic and depression of the 1870s. Trade union membership increased to nearly 200,000 and about half were affiliated to their national unions. The Knights continued to grow but the industrial system was changing. New machinery was introduced to save labor costs, and workers formerly classified and paid as skilled were reduced in wages and status. Large numbers of foreign workers, mostly unskilled, came to America, used to lower standards of living and a less militant pose against their superiors, whether economic, political, or religious. Industrial labor was therefore somewhat easier to recruit and train. The threat of devastating strikes appeared weak since the new industrial worker could be replaced by nonunion, nonstriking workers, or "scabs," who shared with the strikers neither a language nor a heritage of organized conflict. Yet the new economic crisis of 1883 provoked widespread strikes and a rebirth of labor troubles comparable to the '70s but with greater historical significance.

Gompers and other craft leaders were troubled by the indifference if not hostility of the Knights to the new and more effective unionization ideas they practiced. Dual unions, the highest curse one labor organization could shout at another, seemed to flourish because the Knights had such loose and flexible membership requirements. The Cigarmakers were torn by a serious fight between the Gompers–Strasser "pure and simple" leadership and a dissident, or progressive, socialist faction. Other unions were equally disrupted or impatient with the Knights. In late 1881, a "call" by disaffected Knights was made for national unions to meet and form a federation similar to the British one. Gompers was sent as a delegate by the cigarmakers and after a few false starts, the Federation of Organized Trades and Labor Unions of the United States and Canada, was established in November 1881. The Federation announced it was open to both craft and unskilled workers, and that it favored legislation for the immediate relief of certain general problems, which included the unfair competition of convict labor, enforcement of the federal eight-hour law, uniform apprentice rules, total exclusion of Chinese immigrants, free mass education, restriction of child labor, factory inspection laws, union exclusion from conspiracy and liability laws, and a protective tariff. The Federation represented under 25,000 men, had a low and depleting treasury, and was run by an ineffective committee. But it was a threat to the Knights, now led by Terrence V. Powderly, a mediocrity with good intentions, who favored the cooperative movement, opposed strikes, wanted to end the wage system, and had great faith in political action.

Spurred by the threat of the Federation, the Knights joined the wave of strikes which began in 1884. The strikes were lost, broken by stubborn employers who used Pinkerton private detectives and state militias to enforce the absolute power of private property. One prominent railroad strike, against the Jay Gould lines, was won and the Knights took credit for the victory. By the beginning of 1886, the Knights were considered the most powerful labor organization in the country.

In response, the Federation, partly to dramatize their cause, announced a grand plan to enforce a national Eight-Hour-Day Movement to become effective on May 1, 1886. If the rule was not accepted, a general strike would be called by that date. Powderly and the Knights reluctantly joined the movement for eight hours, but secretly advised its assemblies not to participate in the movement or the general strike if called. Gompers spoke in favor of eight hours at a large rally in Union Square. In Chicago, a general strike was partially effective on May 1, but two days later a clash between scabs and strikers led to the killing of four men. The next day a bomb exploded during a meeting in Chicago's Haymarket Square protesting the deaths. The explosion killed and injured dozens of policemen and workers. The Haymarket rally had been organized and encouraged by craft union members who embraced an anarchist philosophy of "terror of the deed," with dynamite advocated as the best and most efficient means of redressing labor's wrongs. All unions were condemned by the hysteria following Haymarket. Anarchism was equated with unionism, and the Knights, the predominant labor organization, took the blame. Before Haymarket, the Knights seemed the worker's hope for the future; after Haymarket, it became an example of the consequences suffered by an organization when intentions exceeded means and undelivered promises smashed false hopes.

Two weeks after Haymarket, Gompers met with a large group of trade union leaders meeting in Philadelphia. These men were not quite proletarian stereotypes. "Practically every man wore a silk hat and a Prince Albert coat," Gompers recalled. "Each [man] was a dignified and self-respecting journeyman who took pride in his trade and his workmanship. Yet we were all poor. Nobody had any money or property." He described the union leaders with affection: "William Weihe, six feet six, the giant puddler; Joseph Wilkinson, the handsome tailor; P. J. McGuire, a lovable and genial companion; Henry Emrich, the eloquent leader of the furniture workers; and Adolph Strasser, the Bismarck of the cigarmakers." The conference proposed a treaty with the Knights calling for peaceful coexistence but in effect granting trade union autonomy within the Knights and limiting the Knights' role to reform and agitation. The Knights refused to accept the terms; negotiations followed but the split became final. In November, the Federation of Organized Trades and Labor Unions became the American Federation of Labor (AFL). Gompers, the chief instigator of craft separation from the Knights, was elected president with a salary of $1,000 a year. He was thirty-six.

The first ten years of the AFL involved a bitter fight for survival against the Knights. Gompers and Powderly despised each other, a hatred basically ideological, but one embittered by racial and religious overtones. Powderly called Gompers "that Christ-slugger" and circulated a "secret" memorandum which said that "the General Executive

Board [of the Knights] has never had the pleasure of seeing Mr. Gompers sober." But the Knights declined in membership and power not because of Gompers' rivalry alone. Two years after the Haymarket disaster, membership dropped from 700,000 to 500,000. Unskilled workers left after the eight-hour disaster; skilled union men either joined the AFL or maintained an independent position. The Knights reorganized, hoping to give craft unions more prominence, but the new structure was no more workable than the old. The failure of "one big union" and the survival of a narrowly based, primarily craft organization had deep historical consequences. The Knights argued in their fight with Gompers that although craft workers deserved more money and consideration, neglect of the unskilled would permit business to use the less talented against more intelligent and skilled workers. Neither side realized that the next half-century of industrial development in America would further modify the production process, greatly reducing specialized functions and creating a huge mass of semi- and unskilled factory workers. The triumph of the Federation and the defeat of the Knights meant that industrialism could advance unhindered by the restraints of mass unionism. Mechanization took command of the armies of labor.

For the nearly forty years of his leadership of the AFL Gompers saw his organization grow from a membership of 140,000 in 1886 to as high as 4,000,000 during the First World War. He lived through the second American Industrial Revolution as well. Gompers was a member of that generation which first used telephones, typewriters, electricity, natural gas, rayon, radio, rubber, and cars. The production ideas of Henry Ford transformed the "modern" factories of Gompers' youth into assembly line wonders. Between 1899 and 1929, the value of machinery, including that of transportation, increased twenty-five times. In the same period oil products increased 880 percent, electrical output 1,900 percent. Vast waves of immigrants, mostly from eastern and southern Europe, crowded into the country. Negroes left the rural oppression of the South in search of a better, urban existence, finding instead Northern indifference. The number of farmers declined rapidly as new equipment permitted fewer men to produce more on less land. Business consolidated along Marxian predictions. By 1904, for example, 185 industrial combinations—or "trusts," "monopolies"—controlled 40 percent of the manufacturing capital in America. By 1930, 1 percent of the banks controlled half of all banking capital.

As head of the largest and most prominent labor organization in this new America, Gompers held surprisingly little authority. He handled the main business of the Federation—relations among and between national affiliates. He was a member of the annually elected executive council and he took most of his instructions from it. He financed organizers hoping to start new unions or locals. He encouraged the establishment of state and city labor federations, lobbied before Congress and state legislatures, petitioned governors and presidents on behalf of labor's cause. He founded and became publisher, editor, and chief writer for the *American Federationist*. His speaking tours around the country were a form of primitive but effective public relations. At plush banquet-meetings of "concerned citizens" he appeared as the talking delegate of the Federation, a deceptively grand symbol of a truly modest organization. But he could not call a strike, start a boycott, or even sign a union contract. He remained in office by gauging the will of the larger craft unions represented on the executive council. Just as the great strength of the AFL lay in its weakness—that is, its flexibility with member unions—so did Gompers appear omnipotent by using limited power boldly.

From 1886 to 1900, Gompers (and the AFL) hoped for survival but planned for expansion. The struggle against the Knights continued and the Order collapsed during the great depression of the '90s. Populism and the possibilities of a farmer–labor coalition were temptations avoided by Gompers. He opposed free silver as a bourgeois phantasy; he rejected the blandishments of bankrupt farmers, claiming that men without houses to mortgage, not "employing farmers," were worthy of his sympathy. He attacked President Cleveland's use of federal troops to break the Pullman strike but he refused to support the strike's leader, Eugene Debs, in his efforts to form an industrial union of all railway workers. He fought the dual unionism of an orthodox Marxist, Daniel DeLeon, and he defeated a socialist program for the collective ownership of the means of production and distribution presented at the 1894 AFL convention. The socialists cleverly maneuvered him out of the presidency but he returned to office the next year. By 1900, the AFL numbered 500,000 workers, the first time in American history that a national labor organization survived an economic slump of such intensity.

After 1900, Gompers, now fifty, shaped his ideas and policies into a mold of enduring strength. For the next twenty-five years his friends and enemies were placed in convenient categories; his rhetoric became familiar and (to some) irritating. The AFL grew but Gompers never changed.

From the Left he was pursued by all the socialist demons Marxism could conjure up. The socialists challenged him at almost every AFL convention. They tried a variety of policies to either 1) "bore from within" the Federation and capture it for their program or 2) create a dual-union situation at every level the AFL reached. In 1898 he condemned socialism as irrelevant to the trade union movement. He denied that members of political parties had standing as authentic delegates to Federation meetings. Thereafter, any socialist hoping to break Gompers' grip over the AFL had to be both a member of an affiliated union and a delegate to the convention. Few socialists met the requirements. But the socialist press hounded him for his failings, for the pure and simple craft exclusivity he preached, for the non-revolutionary pose he took; for the meliorist attitude he publicly favored; and most of all, for the crime of surviving against the force of their opposition. In 1912, after the Socialist party presidential candidate, Debs, polled nearly a million votes, they ran a candidate against Gompers for the AFL presidency, winning nearly a third of the delegate votes. They never came closer to defeating him although a young miner, John L. Lewis did fairly well against him in 1920. To socialists of whatever factional persuasion, Gompers was a labor faker, a disguised capitalist who, with working-class rhetoric, set forth the case for class collaboration.

From the Right, he was hounded by the monied vindictiveness of the National Association of Manufacturers, an AFL with a payroll. The NAM tried to bribe him in 1907, appeared in opposition to his policies at every industrial commission, worked for open-shop legislation on both state and national levels, and in the Bucks Stove case tried to put him in jail. Private detectives, paid for by NAM officials, followed him about from meeting place to saloon. They questioned his patriotism, his race and religion, his honesty, and, primarily, his role. To the NAM, Gompers was more than a socialist. He was an outside agitator, a corruptor of free enterprise, a spokesman for international intrigue, and the enemy of due process and law and order. To most employers, socialism was simply a program advocated by foreign-born cranks who dreamed harmless dreams. The AFL and Gompers were living, realistic nightmares filled with strikes, boycotts, and violence.

However effective the stings from Left and Right, the main enemy of Gompers, and his ambitions for organized labor, came from the harsh impediments of the law. Injunctions to stop union activity before or during a strike were issued by state or federal courts at the request of property owners. Organized labor entered the twentieth century with a criminal record, and for over twenty years Gompers sought full pardon for the prisoners of judicial restraint. The old criminal conspiracy clause of the common law was revived under new licenses of, ironically, the Interstate Commerce Act of 1888 and the Sherman Antitrust Act of 1890, measures designed to limit the excesses of business. In the Pullman strike injunction of 1894 the Supreme Court ruled that "expectant gain" and probable loss by strike action was a civil complaint. A few years later the Court ruled that any person who had actual notice of an injunction was bound by its terms. Thus the "blanket" injunction was born. In the 1900s two cases, the Danbury

Hatters and the Bucks Stove, affected Gompers and all of organized labor. A boycotted firm of hat manufacturers sued the hatters' union for liability and triple damages under the interstate commerce clause of the Sherman Act. The company claimed the boycott was a "conspiracy in restraint of trade" on an interstate basis. The Supreme Court agreed with the company and implied that members were responsible for their union's actions and it further questioned the sheer legality of trades unions. The second case, *Bucks Stove and Range* v. *Gompers et al.* had less judicial significance than personal consequences for Gompers. The metal polishers' union struck the company of an NAM leader, James Van Cleve, in 1906. He ordered an increase in the workday, from nine to ten hours, at his St. Louis plant. The union set up picket lines and started a nationwide boycott of Van Cleve's products. The boycott notice appeared in the *American Federationist*'s "We Don't Patronize" list. Van Cleve applied for and received a federal injunction against the AFL and its officers. In 1907, one year after the injunction was issued, Gompers, John Mitchell, and Frank Morrison were held in contempt of court for violating the terms of the injunction. Gompers received a year in prison, while Morrison and Mitchell got shorter terms. The three AFL officials appealed and lost. But Van Cleve died, the original injunction was overruled as too sweeping, and eventually the new owners of Bucks Stove petitioned the Supreme Court to dismiss the case. Gompers and his colleagues never went to jail. Before 1914, other cases, in lower federal courts, held all strikes illegal under the Sherman Act and in one case against the United Mine Workers, an AFL affiliate, it ruled the union illegal, a remarkable situation for two years until the decision was reversed. The widespread legal campaign against AFL affiliates and personnel had serious consequences for the Federation and its possible growth. But the immediate result for Gompers was that it pushed him into direct political activity in hopes that Congress would amend the Sherman Act.

Gompers entered politics with characteristic enthusiasm and shocking naïveté. In 1906 he presented members of Congress with a list of "Labor's Political Demands," concentrating on amending the Sherman Act as it applied to labor. He threatened Congress with political retaliation if the Peare Anti-Injunction Bill failed to pass. When the bill failed, he launched a campaign to reward the bill's friends and punish its enemies. That failed too. In 1908 he appeared before the platform drafting committee of the Republican party and was insultingly dismissed. The Democrats accepted some features of his program and he actively supported that party's candidate, Bryan, in the presidential campaign. He again appeared before both major parties in 1912 as well as Theodore Roosevelt's Progressive party and in this split race with three major candidates—Taft for the Republicans, Roosevelt, and Woodrow Wilson for the Democrats—he received a somewhat warmer welcome. The victory of Wilson in a narrow election was claimed by Gompers as labor's first presidential success. Wilson agreed to some minor changes in the Sherman Act and he approved the statement that labor was not a commodity under the law. The Clayton Antitrust Act which emerged under Wilson's first administration was hailed by Gompers as labor's magna carta. This boast proved premature. The injunction, though somewhat curbed, still flourished. Other Wilsonian measures—on railway worker regulation and the rights of seamen—were authentic achievements. Gompers became an enthusiast of Wilson especially when the Department of Labor was added to the cabinet and its first Secretary came from the AFL leadership. From loyalty to Wilson and Democrats during the New Freedom, Gompers continued to support that party in national campaigns. But in 1924, near the end of his life, now frustrated by the judicial undermining of the Clayton Act and a resurgence in antilabor effectiveness, he reluctantly pledged the AFL to Robert La Follette's Progressive party campaign. Like most of his political ventures, it failed too, as he knew it would.

Loyalty to Wilson carried him from pacifism to chauvinism during the First World War. When the United States joined the Allies against Germany in 1917 Gompers became an adjunct warlord. He served on advisory boards concerned with industrial affairs and he worked for labor–management peace in the name of the war effort. He tried to use his international labor union contacts to spur on tired Allies. He supported the League of Nations and Wilson's Fourteen Points but was bitterly disappointed when left off the peace conference delegation. Still, he went to Versailles and helped start the International Labor Office. Gompers' war work was not without self-interest for labor. He knew that unionization would increase and it did. Here he followed the precepts of the nineteenth-century French radical Proudhon, who said that "men will willingly die for their countrymen but they won't work for them for nothing." AFL membership soared to nearly 4 million during the holocaust.

The last years of Gompers' life were sad and tragic. He was nearly blind and suffered from Bright's disease. His wife and most cherished daughter died; he remarried unwisely and felt ridicule and pain when this personal union dissolved. The failure to win the great steel strike in 1919 and the loss of many AFL members during the postwar recession exasperated him. Union corruption exposés—officials stealing funds, accepting bribes, blackmailing prospective companies into no-strike deals—embarrassed him. He was older than the key lieutenants who formed his entourage but they too were dated and unimaginative men by this time.

Late in 1924, he collapsed in Mexico City during a meeting of the Pan-American Federation of Labor. A special train rushed his failing body across the Rio Grande into Texas so that he could die on American soil. His friends waited for the end. A brother Mason and vice-president of the AFL, James Duncan, gave Gompers the Masonic grip. The response was faint, but certain. A second ritual handshake was made. Now the response was unclear. A third was made in vain. Characteristically, Gompers died while firmly held by an organizational embrace.

Chronology of the Life of Gompers

1850	(January 27). Born in London, son of Dutch-Jewish cigarmaker.
1863	(July). Emigrates to New York City with parents, joins cigarmakers' union.
1866	(January 28). Marries Sophia Julian.
1869	Knights of Labor founded.
1871	(September). Marches with 25,000 workers in New York demanding eight-hour work day, "Peaceably If We Can, Forcibly If We Must."
1875	(November). Becomes president of New York Local 144, United Cigarmakers. (December). Named organizer for International Cigarmakers Union.
1878	(October). Blacklisted for union activities; cigarmakers locked out in attempt to break union.
1881–83	Divides New York local by ousting socialist faction; lobbies in state legislature for labor and housing reforms.
1881	(November). Helps organize Federation of Organized Trades and Labor Unions modeled on British Trades Union Congress, becomes forerunner of American Federation of Labor (AFL).
1886	(May 1). Speaks at Union Square rally favoring national eight-hour-day movement. (December). Federation of Organized Trades and Labor Unions reorganized as American Federation of Labor; elected president continuing annually (except 1894–95) until death (1924).
1887	(October). Protests scheduled execution of Chicago Haymarket anarchists.
1888	International Association of Machinists founded.
1890	United Mine Workers founded.
1891	(January 9). Appeals to Friedrich Engels over conflicts with socialist rivals.
1892	Homestead Steel strike; twelve workers and Pinkertons killed.
1894	Advises support of AFL political platform, strongly opposing plank 10 demanding "the collective ownership by the people of all means of production and distribution." (September). Pullman Strike (Chicago); protests federal intervention, opposes general strike; defeated for presidency of AFL.

1896	Supports Democratic presidential candidate, William Jennings Bryan and free silver.
1898–1901	Endorses Spanish-American War but attacks American colonial possession of Cuba, Philippines.
1900	AFL membership 548,000.
1901	Becomes vice-president of National Civic Federation led by industrialist Mark Hanna to ameliorate labor–capital disputes.
1906	Submits broad political program to Congress.
1907	With other AFL officers sued by Bucks Stove & Range Company (headed by antiunion president of the National Association of Manufacturers) over labor's right to boycott products of antiunion employer. N.A.M. attempts to bribe him.
1908	Supreme Court rules that unions can be sued under conspiracy provisions of Sherman Antitrust Law (Danbury Hatters Case).
1910	AFL membership 1,562,112.
1911	Aids McNamara bomb case in Los Angeles; shocked when defendants confess guilt.
1912–15	Industrial Commission testimony with socialist Morris Hillguit.
1915	Appeals to Utah Pardon Board to save Joe Hill from execution.
1916	Joins advisory board of the Council of National Defense.
1917	(March 21). Hails formation of Russian Provisional Revolutionary government.
1918	Opposes worker health and unemployment insurance. (July 1). Asks Woodrow Wilson to prevent execution of Tom Mooney. (August 1). Heads steel organizing committee; unionization drive fails.
1919	(January 31). Attends Versailles peace conference. (March 12). Condemns Soviet government.
1919–20	Appeals to Attorney General Palmer for pardon of Eugene Debs, William Haywood, and Emma Goldman, convicted of sedition during World War I.
1919	Urges withdrawal of Allied troops from Russia; opposes trade with and recognition of communist government.
1920	AFL membership 4,078,000; opposes government ownership of railroads.
1924	Endorses Senator Robert M. La Follette as Progressive party presidential candidate. (December 3). Dies in Texas after being stricken while attending conference of Pan-American Federation of Labor in Mexico City; AFL membership 2,865,000.

PART ONE

GOMPERS LOOKS AT THE WORLD

"Never permit sentiment to lead you, but let intellect dominate action."

—C. F. LAURRELL to GOMPERS (1875)

"The trade union is not a Sunday school."

—SAMUEL GOMPERS (1924)

Gompers' life is without significance except as it relates to the history of organized labor in general and the rise of the American Federation of Labor in particular. The selections below trace the gradual change in his thinking from primitive Marxist of the 1870s to quasi-fascist in the 1920s.

1

Cigar-making[1]

Until he became a full-time union official, Gompers worked in the family trade of cigarmaking. "I loved the touch of soft velvety tobacco," he wrote fifty years later, "and gloried in the deft sureness with which I could make cigars grow in my fingers, never wasting a scrap of material. I felt a prince in my own realm with never a care for the future." His miserable working conditions made him an active union organizer but, as one of his employers remarked: "[Gompers] is an agitator, but I don't give a damn, for he makes good cigars."

There was a vast difference between those early unions and the unions of today. Then there was no law or order. A union was a more or less definite group of people employed in the same trade who might

[1] From Samuel Gompers, *Seventy Years of Life and Labor* (New York: E. P. Dutton, 1925), vol. 1, pp. 43–45, 69–70. Reprinted by permission of Augustus M. Kelley Publishers.

help each other out in special difficulties with the employer. There was no sustained effort to secure fair wages through collective bargaining. The employer fixed wages until he shoved them down to a point where human endurance revolted. Often the revolt started by an individual whose personal grievance was sore, who rose and declared: "I am going on strike. All who remain at work are scabs." Usually the workers went out with him.

I remember being busily at work one day when Conrad Kuhn, president of the Cigarmakers' Unions of New York City, entered the shop and announced: "This shop is on strike." Kuhn was a large, fine-looking man, with a stentorian voice that could be heard in every portion of the shop. Without hesitation we all laid down our work and walked out. That was the way it was done in the early days. We had no conception of constructive business tactics beginning with presentation of demands and negotiation to reach an agreement.

Whether we won or lost that strike I don't remember, but the union had no money at the end. Kuhn gave valiant service to us, but his family was actually suffering. It was after the big strike of 1872 that he had to leave the trade. The Turners helped him find a position where he could earn a living, for of course he was black-listed.

The union was generally in a precarious condition financially. Strike funds were never assured, and there were no other benefits. The union represented a feeling of community of burdens of those working in the same industry. It had to acquire a new meaning before it became an industrial agency. It had to strengthen its defensive resources and develop cohesive forces. But that was not only the embryonic stage of unionism; it was the fledgling period of industry. Industrial production was uncouth, unscientific, just about as planless as unionism. Management, accountancy, salesmanship, elimination of waste were in the rule-of-thumb stage. Factory architecture and industrial sanitation were undeveloped sciences.

Any kind of an old loft served as a cigar shop. If there were enough windows, we had sufficient light for our work; if not, it was apparently no concern of the management. There was an entirely different conception of sanitation both in the shop and in the home of those days from now. The toilet facilities were a water-closet and a sink for washing purposes, usually located by the closet. In most cigar shops our towels were the bagging that came around the bales of Havana and other high grades of tobacco. Cigar shops were always dusty from the tobacco stems and powdered leaves. Benches and work tables were not designed to enable the workmen to adjust bodies and arms comfortably to work surface. Each workman supplied his own cutting board of lignum vitae and knife blade.

The tobacco leaf was prepared by strippers who drew the leaves from the heavy stem and put them in pads of about fifty. The leaves had to be handled carefully to prevent tearing. The craftsmanship of the cigarmaker was shown in his ability to utilize wrappers to the best advantage to shave off the unusable to a hairbreadth, to roll so as to cover holes in the leaf and to use both hands so as to make a perfectly shaped and rolled product. These things a good cigarmaker learned to do more or less mechanically, which left us free to think, talk, listen, or sing. I loved the freedom of that work, for I had earned the mind-freedom that accompanied skill as a craftsman. I was eager to learn from discussion and reading or to pour out my feeling in song. Often we chose someone to read to us who was a particularly good reader, and in payment the rest of us gave him sufficient of our cigars so he was not the loser. The reading was always followed by discussion, so we learned to know each other pretty thoroughly. We learned who could take a joke in good spirit, who could marshal his thoughts in an orderly way, who could distinguish clever sophistry from sound reasoning. The fellowship that grew between congenial shopmates was something that lasted a lifetime. . . .

Anyone who does not know the cigarmaking trade will find it diffi-cult to appreciate the educational value of the little forum existing in each shop. It gave education in such a way as to develop personality, for in no other place were we so wholly natural. The nature of our work developed a camaraderie of the shop such as few workers enjoy. It was a world in itself—a cosmopolitan world. Shopmates came from everywhere—some had been nearly everywhere. When they told us of strange lands and peoples, we listened eagerly. No one ever questioned another as to his past life, for many were revolutionists who sought new opportunity and safety by leaving the past blank.

2
Early Radicalism[1]

In 1871, Gompers joined a New York City rally demanding the eight-hour work day. Red flags and banners were carried by the crowd proclaiming: "EIGHT HOURS FOR WORK, EIGHT HOURS FOR REST, EIGHT HOURS FOR WHAT WE WILL," and "PEACEABLY IF WE CAN, FORCIBLY IF WE MUST." Two years later the depression of '73 forced more than a third of all New York employees out of work. In January 1874 a huge rally was held in Tompkins Square demanding relief for the unemployed, food and lodgings for the destitute. Armed, mounted police charged the peaceable crowd and dispersed them with mindless brutality. A radical newspaper condemned the police action: "When organized labor asks for bread or rather a means to make bread you must not offer it a stone. Or if you do, it will take the stone only to hurl it back to you."

I reached the Square a little after ten. It had been a drill field and playground and, though a bit out of repair, was commonly used by the working people for general gatherings and speeches. A high iron fence surrounded the park with wide gate entrances. Soon the park was packed and all the avenues leading to it crowded. The people were quiet. There was nothing out of harmony with the spirit of friendly conferences between the chief public official and workless and breadless citizens. The gathering was planned as visible proof of suffering and destitution among New York unemployed. A paper was edited for this special meeting by Lucien Sanial and P. J. McGuire. The paper, widely circulated among the unemployed, the working people, and the city authorities, contained the program proposed by the workers. The *Volcano* was also conspicuously for sale. Tom-ri-John, everybody in New York in the early 'seventies will remember as a Communist or Socialist or a reformer of some kind. Tom was also a journalistic reformer. He ran a newspaper called the *Volcano*. It was printed on bright yellow paper and its articles set up in red ink. In accord with their distribution of family responsibility, it was Mrs. Tom-

[1] Ibid., pp. 95–98.

ri-John's business to sell these papers, and her working dress (masculine garb) served to attract attention while the big stick she always carried was her rod and staff of defense and support. The couple had three children—Eruptor, Vesuvia, and Emancipator.

It was about 10:30 when a detachment of police surrounded the park. Hardly had they taken position before a group of workers marched into the park from Avenue A. They carried a banner bearing the words "TENTH WARD UNION LABOR." Just after they entered the park the police sergeant led an attack on them. He was followed by police mounted and on foot with drawn night-sticks. Without a word of warning they swept down the defenseless workers, striking down the standard-bearer and using their clubs right and left indiscriminately on the heads of all they could reach.

Shortly afterwards the mounted police charged the crowd on Eighth Street, riding them down and attacking men, women, and children without discrimination. It was an orgy of brutality. I was caught in the crowd on the street and barely saved my head from being cracked by jumping down a cellarway. The attacks of the police kept up all day long—wherever the police saw a group of poorly dressed persons standing or moving together. Laurrell went to Tompkins Square and received a blow from the police across his back, the effect of which remained with him for several months.

The next few days disclosed revolting stories of police brutality inflicted on the sick, the lame, the innocent bystander. Mounted police and guards had repeatedly charged down crowded avenues and streets. A reign of terror gripped that section of the city. To this day I cannot think of that wild scene without my blood surging in indignation at the brutality of the police on that day. They justified their policy by the charge that Communism was rearing its head. The Internationals replied with the ugly charge that they had been sold out by George Blair and others of the Workingmen's Union who they said had told the authorities that they were dynamiters trying to organize a Commune, a charge that never died until it was thrashed out in the Central Labor Union years later and Blair exonerated. Blair was a boxmaker by trade and was then operating a co-operative establishment. He was an ardent Knight of Labor which then, of course, was a wholly secret body. I always thought him honest and loyal to the best interests of labor. He did not look with friendliness upon any attempt to turn the labor movement into opera bouffe. He may have asked for police protection to have the workers properly protected— but I am perfectly confident he betrayed no trust.

The Tompkins Square outrage was followed by a period of extreme repression. The New York police borrowed continental methods of espionage. Private indoor meetings were invaded and summarily ended by the ejection of those present. The police frustrated several meetings held to protest against police brutality and in defense of the right of free assemblage for a lawful purpose.

I was in no way connected with the arrangement of this demonstration and was present as an intensely interested working man and the import of the situation bore in upon me. As the fundamentals came to me, they became guide-posts for my understanding of the labor movement for years to come. I saw how professions of radicalism and sensationalism concentrated all the forces of organized society against a labor movement and nullified in advance normal, necessary activity. I saw that leadership in the labor movement could be safely entrusted only to those into whose hearts and minds had been woven the experiences of earning their bread by daily labor. I saw that betterment for workingmen must come primarily through workingmen. I saw the danger of entangling alliances with intellectuals who did not understand that to experiment with the labor movement was to experiment with human life. I realized too that many of those of the radical, revolutionary impatient group were of the labor movement and just as sincere as many of those whose judgment was more dependable. The labor movement is made up of men and women of all sorts of natures and experiences. Their welfare depends on solidarity—one group cannot sit in judgment upon others or condemn publicly, but all must do what they can for mutual protection. Division is the great hazard of the labor movement.

3

Haymarket Petition (1887)[1]

The Haymarket explosion in May 1886 killed the eight-hour movement as well as a number of policemen and demonstrators. After the rump trial of the Chicago anarchists, Gompers petitioned the governor of Illinois, seeking a reprieve for the men sentenced to death. T. V. Powderly, the head of the Knights of Labor, feared associating the Knights with the condemned radicals. "Better that seven times seven men hang," he wrote just before their execution, "than to hang a millstone of odium around the standard of this Order." "Anarchism," he concluded, "was un-American."

In the twentieth century, Gompers intervened on behalf of I.W.W. leaders being tried for the assassination of a western governor; he defended the McNamara brothers (until their confession) in the Los Angeles Times *bombing case (1911), and he pleaded in vain with President Woodrow Wilson, and later with success with President Harding, for the release of Debs, Emma Goldman, and others convicted of seditious activities during the First World War.*

But the ghost of the Haymarket bomb haunted Gompers throughout his career. Every act of labor terrorism during his lifetime somehow brushed his reputation.

To the Governor of Illinois:

I have differed all my life with the principles and methods of the condemned, but know no reason why I should not ask the Governor to interpose and save condemned men from the gallows. The execution would not be one of justice; not to the interest of the great state of Illinois; not to the interests of the country; nor the workingmen. I come as a representative of the New York Central Labor Union and as president of the American Federation of Labor, organizations opposed to anarchy.

If these men are executed it would simply be an impetus to this

[1] From *AFL History, Encyclopedia, and Reference Book* (Washington, D. C., 1924), p. 73.

so-called revolutionary movement which no other thing on earth can give. These men would, apart from any consideration of mercy or humanity, be looked upon as martyrs. Thousands and thousands of labor men all over the world would consider that these men had been executed because they were standing up for free speech and free press.

We ask you, sir, to interpose your great power to prevent so dire a calamity. If this great country could be great and magnanimous enough to grant amnesty to Jeff Davis, it ought to be great and magnanimous enough to grant clemency to these men.

The workingmen of the country, the people of the country even apart from the workingmen, have their eyes centered upon you. The eyes not only of the people of this country but of the entire world are directed toward Springfield, Ill. We have found that throughout the length and breadth of the civilized world wherever an opportunity exists for the people to manifest their wishes they have protested strongly the execution of the sentence and ask, sir, that the only power that can intervene between these men and death—the hand of Governor Oglesby—be exercised to stand between them. The working people have long begged for justice and very frequently not in vain. They arise now and ask in the name of mercy, in the name of humanity, in the name of progress, not to allow this execution to take place, but, sir, to stand between these men and death, and as I in a letter and dispatch sent to you have said, you will not only be blessed by the country but the unborn thousands that come after us.

I want to say to you, sir, I am not desirous of going into the details of the question. I don't believe I am competent to do so; but I believe that in some measure, however remote, the police of Chicago have been somewhat responsible for this trouble. I ask myself what good can come to the people of the state of Illinois; what good can come to the people of our country; what good can come to the good name of our country and people if these men are executed? Are we not strong enough, and intelligent enough to protect our lives and interests as a people without the execution of these men? I cannot conceive what possible good results the execution of these men will have upon society.

4
What Does Labor Want?

Having survived the Haymarket affair the most critical years of the AFL extended throughout the depression of the 1890s. "Homestead" and "Pullman" were two of the more promi-nent names in a crisis decade. Gompers' rhetoric eventually moderated but the remnants of his earlier Marxism are made clear in his pamphlet What Does Labor Want? *(1893).*

PRIMITIVE MARXISM [1]

What does labor want? It wants the earth and the fulness thereof. There is nothing too precious, there is nothing too beautiful, too lofty, too ennobling, unless it is within the scope and comprehension of labor's aspirations and wants.

Modern society . . . is based on one simple fact, the practical sepa-ration of the capitalistic class from the great mass of the industrious.

The separation between the capitalistic class and the laboring mass is not so much a difference in industrial rank as it is a difference in social status, placing the laborers in a position involving a degradation of mind and body.

A distinction scarcely noticed earlier has become a veritable chasm, economic, social and moral. On each side of this seemingly impassable chasm we see the hostile camps of the rich and poor. On one side, a class in possession of all the tools and means of labor; on the other an immense mass begging for the opportunity to labor. In the mansion the soft notes betokening ease and security; in the tenement, the stifled wail of drudgery and poverty, the arrogance of the rich ever mounting in proportion to the debasement of the poor. . . .

The capitalist class had its origins in force and fraud, that it has maintained and extended its brutal sway more or less directly through the agency of specified legislation, most ferocious and barbarous, but always in cynical disregard of all law save its own arbitrary will. . . .

This class of parasites devours incomes derived from many sources,

[1] From Samuel Gompers, *What Does Labor Want?* (New York, 1893), pp. 6–10.

from the stunted babies employed in the mills, mines and factories to the lessees of the gambling halls and the profits of fashionable brothels; from the lands which the labor of others had made valuable; from the royalties on coal and other miners beneath the surface and from rent of houses above the surface.

5
Craft vs. Industrial Unionism[1]

A long and bitter argument developed around the question of organizational forms. Gompers, like most founders of the AFL, insisted that workers be unionized by craft or specialty since these "skilled" workers were more intelligent and already better paid than the semiskilled or unskilled; and that their craft consciousness developed a bond of enduring strength against employers. Much of the argument between craft and industrial workers was misleading, since the AFL included miners and seamen. But repeated attempts—in 1901 and 1919—to organize steel workers failed and during Gompers' time and until the New Deal, "organized labor" meant skilled or specialized labor.

The attempt to force the trade unions into what has been termed industrial organization is perversive of the history of the labor movement, runs counter to the best conceptions of the toilers' interests now, and is sure to lead to the confusion which precedes dissolution and disruption. It is time for the American Federation of Labor to solemnly call a halt. It is time for our fellow-unionists entrusted with the grave responsibilities to help stem the tide of expansion madness lest either by their indifference or encouragement their organizations will be drawn into the vortex that will engulf them to their possible dismemberment and destruction. There is virtue and a great need of praise due in organizing our fellow-workers that they may defend and further their interests. No tribute too great can be paid those engaged in the past and in the present who have done and who are doing this splendid work; but virtue, merit, and tribute must be effaced unless we meet the conditions, aye, the awful calamity which is inevitable if trade union lines are not recognized and enforced—enforced not so much by an edict of this Federation, but by the common sense and power of the organizations themselves. The advocates of the so-called industrial system of labor organizations urge that an effective strike can only be conducted when all workmen, regardless of trade, calling,

[1] From *AFL History, Encyclopedia, and Reference Book* (Washington, D. C., 1919), pp. 246–47.

or occupation, are affected. That this is not borne out by the history of strikes in the whole labor movement is easily demonstrable. Though here and there such strikes have been temporarily successful, in the main they have been fraught with injury to all. The so-called industrial system of organization implies sympathetic strikes, and these time and experience have demonstrated, that as a general proposition they should be discarded, while strikes of particular trades or callings have had the largest number of successes and the minimum of defeats. Quite apart from these considerations, however, are the splendid advantages obtained by the trade unions without the necessity of strikes or the interruption of industry. No one will attempt to say that a sympathetic strike shall under no circumstances occur. Under certain conditions it may be not only justifiable but practical and successful, even if only as an emphatic protest against a great injustice or wrong; but generally and normally considered, such strikes can not be of advantage. One feature in connection with a system of industrial organization and its concomitant, the sympatheic strike, has been overlooked. By its methods any one of our international organizations could be financially drained and actually ruined in a very brief period in an effort to sustain the members involved: while, on the other hand, in a well-formulated trade union movement, a large number of men of different crafts, belonging to their own respective international trade unions, could be indefinitely sustained financially and victory achieved. At least the organizations maintained, not only to continue that battle, but to take up the cudgels in defense of their members elsewhere. The advocates of the industrial system of organization undertake to correct an error by the commission of a graver one, the failure of our international trade unions to primarily provide themselves with large funds to protect their own members and to assist their fellow-unionists of other trades when they are engaged in conflict. . . .

6

On Populism[1]

At the founding meeting in 1874 of the abortive Work-
ingman's party, one speaker proclaimed: "Workingmen, laborers,
come in solid phalanx, unite with your brethren in the Country."
The radical hope of a farmer–labor coalition was never realized
in America. Attempts were made to form a unified political front
—between the various worker organizations and the populists—
but the results were invariably poor. Gompers was initially hos-
tile to populism and free silver but he eventually supported Wil-
liam Jennings Bryan in his three unsuccessful presidential cam-
paigns (1896, 1900, and 1908). Gompers' opposition to the farm-
ers' cause was stated in almost classical Marxian terms: "I say that
I have sympathy," he told a friend in 1893, "with those who have
a little land and a little house burdened by mortgage, but I am
compelled by my observations . . . to spend my largest sum of
sympathy on those who have neither land nor house to mortgage."
The populists, Gompers often remarked, were "employing farm-
ers," capitalists of the land. Thereafter, he tried to establish farm-
worker locals, but the organizing campaigns usually failed.
He contributed the following article during the first major na-
tional populist campaign of 1892.

It is with some trepidation that I begin writing this article, for
while it may be true that I have as good opportunities as any other
man in the country of conjecturing the probable action of the workingmen of America, and particularly those affiliated with the American
Federation of Labor in the coming Presidential campaign. . . .

Why should its attitude be different in the coming Presidential campaign from what it has been in the past? In what way does the coming
campaign differ from those of 1876, 1880, 1884 or 1888? Is there any
particular principle involved in the party issues in which the wage-
workers have a deep or keen interest? There is indeed none.

Was there any real improvement or deterioration in the condition

[1] From Samuel Gompers, "Organized Labor in the Campaign," *North American Review* 155 (July 1892): 91–96.

of the working people, as a result of the changes, when Mr. Cleveland succeeded the late Mr. Arthur, or when Mr. Harrison succeeded Mr. Cleveland? I think not, and I feel satisfied that I will not lose my reputation as a "prophet" if I venture to predict that, so far as the wage-workers are concerned, it will matter little if President Harrison or some other Republican on the one side, or any member of the Democratic party on the other, should be elected to succeed the present incumbent, or even should the People's Party succeed (though I doubt that they even entertain the belief that they will succeed) in electing their candidate to the Presidency.

The members of the organizations affiliated with the Federation will no doubt, in a large measure, as citizens, vote for the candidate of the party of their own political predilections. But the number is ever on the increase who disenthral themselves from partisan voting and exercise their franchise to reward or chastise those parties and candidates, that deserve either their friendship or resentment. With us it is not a question of parties or men; it is a question of measures.

That there exists a feeling of dissatisfaction with, and bitter antagonism to, both the Republican and Democratic parties is not to be gainsaid. Broken promises to labor, insincere, half-hearted support and even antagonism of legislation in the interest of the toilers on the one hand, and the alacrity and devotion with which the interests of the corporations and the wealth-possessing class are nurtured, protected and advanced on the other, have had their effect, and the result is that many toilers have forever severed their connection with the old parties. That the number will continue to grow larger year by year I have not the slightest doubt. To me this party defection of the wage-workers is one of the signs of the dawn of a healthier public opinion, a sturdier manhood and independence, and a promise to maintain the liberties that the people now enjoy, as well as to ever struggle on to attain that happy goal towards which, throughout its entire history, the human family have been perpetually pushing forward.

But in leaving the old parties, to whom, to what shall former Democratic or Republican workmen turn? To the People's Party? Are such changes and improvements promised there that the workers can with any degree of assurance throw in their political fortunes with that party? Of course, acting upon the principle "of all evils choose the least," they will more generally coöperate with the People's Party than with any similar party heretofore gracing the Presidential political arena.

As a matter of fact, however, to support the People's Party under the belief that it is a *labor* party is to act under misapprehension. It is not and cannot, in the nature of its make-up, be a labor party, or even one in which the wage-workers will find their haven. Composed, as the People's Party is, mainly of *employing* farmers without any regard to the interests of the *employed* farmers of the country districts or the mechanics and laborers of the industrial centres, there must of necessity be a divergence of purposes, methods, and interests.

In speaking thus frankly of the composition of the People's Party there is no desire to belittle the efforts of its members, or even to withhold the sympathy due them in their agitation to remedy the wrongs which they suffer from corporate power and avarice; on the contrary, the fullest measure of sympathy and all possible encouragement should and will be given them; for they are doing excellent work in directing public attention to the dangers which threaten the body politic of the republic. But, returning to the consideration of the entire coöperation or amalgamation of the wage-workers' organizations with the People's Party, I am persuaded that all who are more than superficial observers, or who are keen students of the past struggles of the proletariat of all countries, will with one accord unite in declaring the union impossible, because it is unnatural. Let me add that, before there can be any hope of the unification of labor's forces of the field, farm, factory, and workshop, the people who work on and in them for wages must be organized to protect *their* interests against those who pay them wages for that work.

Then, if as an organization, the American Federation of Labor will take no official part in the coming Presidential campaign of a partisan character, it may, with a fair degree of reason, be asked what we will do? Some have asked whether we will have a candidate of our own in the field. I can answer both by saying that, apart from the acts already referred to above, we shall maintain as a body a masterly inactivity. As organized trade-unionists, we have had some experience with a Presidential candidate, and in campaigns of our own, the lessons of which have not been forgotten by us.

It may not be generally known that in 1872 the organized workingmen of the country placed a candidate in nomination for the Presidency of the United States. The National Labor Union, the immediate predecessor and parent of the Federation, at its convention of that year, held in Columbus, O., selected the late David Davis, of Illinois, as its standard bearer. So far as the nomination was concerned, quite a degree of success was attained. A candidate was placed in the field, but it was at the cost of the life of the organization. Another convention of the National Labor Union was never held after that. Indeed, so great was the reaction among the organized workingmen against this departure, and so thoroughly had they lost confidence in a general organization of a national character, that, despite all efforts to induce them to be represented in a national convention, defeat and disappointment were the result until 1881, when the Federation was called into existence.

Since its organization the American Federation of Labor has kept in mind two facts: first, the lamentable experience of its predecessor; and second, that, in the struggle for improved conditions and emancipation for the toilers, what is wanted is the organization of the wage-workers, not on "party" lines, but on the lines of their class interests.

As an organization, the American Federation of Labor is not in harmony either with the existing or projected political parties. So deep-seated is the conviction in this matter that, long ago, it was decided to hold the conventions of the Federation *after* the elections. Thus freed from party bias and campaign crimination, these gatherings have been in a position to declare for general principles, and to judge impartially upon the merits or demerits of each party, holding each to an accountability for its perfidy to the promises made to the working people, and at the same time keeping clear and distinct the economic character of the organization. By our non-political partisan character as an organization, we tacitly declare that political liberty with economic independence is illusory and deceptive, and that only in so far as we gain economic independence can our political liberty become tangible and important. This may sound like political heresy, but it is economic truth. . . .

Having mapped out our course, the members of the American Federation of Labor can look on the coming Presidential campaign with a degree of equanimity not often attained by the average citizen. The excitement and turmoil, criminations and recriminations will not rend our organization asunder, as it has done so many others; and during it all, and when the blare of trumpets has died away, and the "spell-binders" have received their rewards, the American Federation of Labor will still be found plodding along, doing noble battle in the struggle for the uplifting of the toiling masses.

7
Parliamentarian

Annual conventions of the AFL were organized and controlled by Gompers and his staff. Opponents called him a "dictator" and manipulator of these proceedings. The following selections show a) Gompers in action at the 1896 meeting, debating the Cuban question and listing a few achievements of the Federation for the year; and b) a convention squabble between Gompers and some socialist opponents in 1912, the last year his presidency was seriously threatened from the Left.

THE CUBAN QUESTION (1896) [1]

Resolutions

By Delegates McNeil, Elliot, McGuire, McBride, Yarnell, Gompers, Keough, Dernell, Weismann, Valentine, Lennon.

RESOLVED, That the American Federation of Labor in convention assembled, hereby tenders its hearty sympathy to all men struggling against oppression, and especially to the men of Cuba who for years have sacrificed and suffered to secure the right of self-government.

RESOLVED, That the example of the people of France, in giving recognition and aid to the Fathers in their struggle to secure the independence of the colonies, is worthy of imitation, and we hereby call upon the President and Congress to recognize the belligerent rights of the Cuban revolutionists.

Delegate Black thought it outside our jurisdiction. He was in hearty sympathy with the Cubans, but we should confine ourselves to our own particular and peculiar functions.

Delegate Meyer spoke briefly in the affirmative.

Delegate O'Donnell was also in favor, was surprised at the statements of the previous speaker. The President of the United States should be censured for his negligence. The Cubans were making a magnificent struggle and should be supported.

Delegate White said we were talking of organizing and fraternizing

[1] *Reports of the AFL Convention Proceedings*, 1893–96, pp. 51–52.

35

with the workers in other lands. Co-operation with the Cubans was necessary to take them out of the clutches of Spain.

Delegate Weismann said he signed the resolution for purely humanitarian purposes. The bloodshed would not cease until the throne of Spain was repudiated.

President Gompers spoke at length in the affirmative. The independence of the Cubans is essential to their economic organization. Liberty, truth, and freedom [were] the basis of the make-up of the world. It must be obtained before the Cuban proletariat could be organized. He was a trade-unionist in America and England but he would be a socialist in Germany, and in Russia a Nihilist. He had the honor of correspondence with the representatives of the Cubans, as well as personal acquaintance. Liberty and freedom should prevail. It was necessary for the different classes interested in Cuba to unite to achieve their purpose just the same as it was for the wage-workers to unite with the capitalists in baronial times. He wanted peace and would fight for it. It was necessary to step in and stop this butchery once and for all.

Delegate Donnelly entered a protest to such action. It appeared to him that in presenting resolutions for liberty, we should first remember that we want liberty at home, higher wages and shorter hours.

Delegate Yarnell looked to the labor movement for the ultimate emancipation of the wage-workers, but was not so narrow as to think we could not stretch out a helping hand to Cuba. It was our duty to adopt the resolution and show that the breath of liberty still lived in the breasts of American workmen. We want to show Spain that when she brings her minions to murder on American soil, she will meet with the condemnation of the American people. It was time we asked Congress to interfere. The president was cowardly in his non-recognition of Cuba, and should be censured.

Delegate Furuseth said he felt sorry he must run counter to the older heads, but he did not see that the question of Cuba had much to do with liberty; would prefer the question had not been brought up. There was enough feeling in the United States to justify the executive officers to throw a firebrand that would involve, perhaps, the loss of a quarter million of people. A war between the United States and Spain would not be one of days but of months, must be conducted on water and finally, perhaps, on the Spanish continent. When the war was over and Cuba a republic, then what have we gained? A national debt as large as the one we have now, an army never rid of and a navy as well. For these reasons he would not add to the flame already burning as to whom should not rob the Cubans.

Delegate Black arose to a question of privilege. He deemed it his privilege to voice his views without recrimination as had been done. He was evidently not alone in the position he had taken.

The resolution was adopted by 60 to 9.

Delegate Weissmann desired to state that he signed the resolutions, but discussion had changed his opinion.

The President desired the following to be placed upon the records:

New York, December 14, 1896.

To the American Federation of Labor, Mr. Samuel Gompers, President, Cincinnati, O.

Dear Sir:—"The American Friends of Cuba," an organization founded for the purpose of aiding and assisting the Cuban people in their struggle for liberty, appeal to you in the vast army of organized labor in their behalf.

To you whom are struggling for economic liberty, an oppressed people turn their eyes and ask you to aid them that they may enjoy political liberty. The influence of organized labor thrown into the scale will outweigh any other interest that may be placed against it, and surely the influence of organized labor will be cast with the oppressed and against the oppressor. It is unnecessary for me to recite the many deeds of outrage and inhumanity committed by the Spanish Government upon the Cuban people. They are recorded in the press every day. Rape, arson and murder have been committed in order that Spain may continue to rule a people by whom she is despised.

We ask you to join with us in a petition to Congress that we may put a stop to those atrocities. We ask you to make an official declaration of sympathy with the Cuban people and forward the same to Congress, as coming from you, representing as you do, the bone and sinew of the land, it will give to Congress the confidence that is needed.

We send you a few blank petitions which we would ask you to circulate among your delegates for signatures, and shall upon request from you or any delegate forward as many others as may be desired.

Hoping that the American Federation of Labor may look upon this matter favorably and wishing it and its members success in their efforts to aid the toiling masses, I remain,

Very respectfully yours,
FRANZ MAYER, President,
538 E. 87th St.

Achievements

Sufficient has been secured to give a fair idea of the work that is being done, from which it will be observed that considerable progress has been made, notwithstanding the poor industrial conditions that prevailed. No figures can be compiled of the results achieved without disagreement; that is, of the reductions and other encroachments prevented by the fact of being organized; as one of those reporting put it, "by the silent power of unity."

Tailors.—Won fourteen strikes and lockouts, compromised [2] eight, lost nine. Increased the wages of 911 members from 3 to 10 percent.

[2] Settled—Ed.

There were seventeen lockouts on account of reductions in wages averaging 15 percent, involving 721 members; a settlement was made on an average of 6 percent; altogether there were 1,632 persons involved. In nineteen cities reductions were prevented, and in five advances were made without strikes, involving 1,823 members.

Bakers.—Won two strikes, compromised two, lost one. Gains, $2.00 per week and reduction of one hour, benefiting 750 persons, while none were injured. Six boycotts were placed, and three are still on.

Molders.—Won six strikes, compromised four, lost two, pending four; twelve were for wages paid in 1892. An average advance of 10 percent was gained, benefiting 297 persons. Besides this, every attempt to reduce wages was successfully resisted. By conferring with the Stove Founders' National Defense Association they have maintained the piece price for stove molding prevailing in 1892.

Granite Cutters.—Won fourteen strikes, three pending, lost none. Increased wages slightly in ten instances, and secured permanent recognition for union in six. Lost nothing; benefited 2,380 persons. Also made, without strikes, regular yearly settlement for union wages, hours and regular pay-days, and eliminated largely "no-discrimination-against-union-men" clause, only a few of such remaining.

Cigarmakers.—Won thirty strikes, compromised fifteen, lost six. Benefited 653 persons, and 83 worsted. General scale of wages and hours maintained.

Elastic Goring Weavers.—No strikes or lockouts. Settled by conference price list on new grade of work and minor matters.

Tobacco Workers.—No strikes or lockouts. Settled minor matters by conference. Have gained great advantage through their label. Have trouble pending with the trust.

Hatters.—No strikes or lockouts. Four factories unionized by the label, and won two boycotts.

Stove Mounters.—Won one strike, compromised four, benefited 62 persons.

Slate Quarrymen.—No strikes or lockouts. General situation unchanged.

Harness and Saddlemakers.—Compromised one strike, benefiting 11 persons. No losses.

Patternmakers.—Won one strike, lost one; benefited twenty-four, and six worsted. Much accomplished without trouble in raising minimum rates, shop considerations, time and a half for overtime, and the complete abolition of piece-work.

Brewery Workers.—Do not strike. Won two boycotts; several pending. Benefited 60 people. Have made good advances in organizing.

Barbers.—No difficulties; general progress.

Garment Workers.—Won two strikes, compromised one, lost three. In Baltimore, Chicago and Cincinnati manufacturers combined because of strike in one shop. Involved 10,200 members. Defeated after stubborn contest through trade dullness. In Chicago some tailoring branches won; cutters lost. In Philadelphia 1,000 members secured a reduction of three hours per day, but subsequently lost it owing to extreme dullness. In New York and Brooklyn thirteen unions of 12,000 members secured signed agreements with a security cash forfeit in the event of violation. Almost complete trade depression caused inroads upon conditions prevailing, but largely prevented and numerous concessions gained. In the overall branch wages raised and hours reduced without trouble, benefiting 1,200.

Machinists.—Won fifteen strikes, lost two, benefited 2,450 persons and worsted 550. One thousand men in Cleveland secured Saturday half holiday, time-and-a-half for overtime, and representation when having a grievance. Conditions in Joliet and Easton better since the strike than ever before. Obtained increase in wages in eight sections, and successfully resisted reductions in fifteen. Won two boycotts and one pending. Reduced piece-work system to its lowest possible minimum; prevented the introduction of running two machines and the displacement of machinists by handy men. Brown Hoisting strike still on; men have secured other positions. So at Illinois Steel Co. and Ingersoll-Sergeant Drill Co. conditions generally vastly improved. If figured out would show a benefit of over one million dollars.

Printing Pressmen.—Won three strikes, lost four, benefited 39 persons, worsted 41. Made gains without difficulties in Minneapolis, New York City and Chicago.

Mineral Miners.—Secured increase of 10 percent in one mine and a six months' trial of the eight-hour day, which is working satisfactorily.

Printers.—Won forty-five strikes, compromised three, lost eighteen, four unsettled. Benefited 844 persons and 225 were worsted. (From February 9.)

Horseshoers.—Won six strikes, lost none. Secured nine-hour day in thirteen cities; without strike in six. Benefited 300 persons.

Iron and Steel Workers.—Had several strikes, one still pending. Secured an advance of 12½ percent in an important branch for several thousands of our members. Successfully resisted a strongly pressed reduction. No losses.

Brotherhood of Carpenters and Joiners.—Won ninety-eight strikes, compromised eleven, lost seven. Secured eight-hour plan in twenty-four more cities, and nine hours in thirteen cities. Twelve percent of membership lost from about 15 to 20 percent in wages. Building trade prostrate.

Street Railway Employees.—Won one strike, lost one; one lockout, still unsettled. Has been a poor year for organizations. Secured an advance without trouble.

Longshoremen.—Won twelve strikes, compromised two, lost none. Organized twenty-seven local unions. Secured an average increase of 20 percent along the lakes. Along the coast prevented reduction.

Seamen.—Increased wages on the lakes, 50 cents per day; on the coast remain the same.

THE NATIONAL CIVIC FEDERATION DEFENDED (1911) [3]

Is there any one who seriously believes that the men in the American labor movement, the officers of the American Federation of Labor and the officers of the International Typographical Union, or the Street Railway men, the Firemen and others, are not glad of the opportunity to testify to the work done by the Civic Federation in behalf of their organizations? Is there any one who imagines for a minute that these men, my colleagues on the Executive Council and myself, can be chloroformed or hypnotized by anything an opponent of organized labor may say or do? I venture to say that except as a figure of speech, except as it is intended to prejudice the mind of the uninformed, not one of those who have introduced the resolutions really believes it.

In the meetings of the National Civic Federation, if I may go so far as to say it, not only for others but certainly for myself, I think we have been more radical and persistent in our utterances than we would have been in the meeting rooms of any of our unions. I don't know that I could find language in my vocabulary to more strongly present the claims of labor, the rights of labor, or to portray as best I could the wrongs from which labor suffers than I have in the meetings of the National Civic Federation. I challenge any man here now to point to one utterance of mine in the National Civic Federation that he will challenge as a trades unionist, that he will question as to its accuracy and its insistence.

But there is another phase of it. Ask—no, you need not ask, the statement will be volunteered by Socialists—that "after all your trade union activity, after all your trades unions are played out institutions, your strikes and boycotts are played out, they are obsolete weapons, what is the use of them? Vote right, and you will vote yourself into glory and salvation!" And how strange it is for those who so insistently claim that trade union activity is futile, and yet charge us with being

[3] *Reports of the Proceedings of the Thirty-first Annual Convention of the AFL* (November 1911).

chloroformed on the industrial field! If the strike and the boycott are obsolete and useless, where is the danger of chloroforming us in our conferences with the employers? For it is those things which we primarily and principally discuss.

The idea upon which that claim of the uselessness of trade union activity, the strike and the boycott, are declared to be obsolete, is this: When trade unions increase wages the Socialists say "employers of labor will put up prices higher than really the wages that you have secured are increased." If such a statement were founded upon facts it would be in the interests of the employing class to concede every demand for an increase in wages which we make. The truth is that frequently prices are increased about the same time, or shortly after, frequently before an increase in wages is secured. I imagined that Socialists no longer believe what LaSalle laid down as the "Iron Law of Wages." That has been disregarded by even as much intelligence as the average Socialist can acquire. . . .

The Civic Federation! Has it done anything for labor? I want to say here and now that personally I have profited not one dollar by my association with the National Civic Federation. I would lose not one cent if I severed my connection with it. As a rule it is not necessary to use even the good offices of the National Civic Federation for me to obtain an interview with almost any man in America. I seem to have at least sufficient of the respect of the people in all walks of life to secure any personal interview I may want, but my only desire for an opportunity for a conference is to discuss some concrete proposition in which the men and women of labor are interested.

Has the National Civic Federation done anything?

I shall not attempt to discuss the various propositions in regard to trade disputes, the conferences secured and the adjustments reached. I should prefer that others, when the time may come, if not now, some time in the future, shall tell the story. I want to deal with a few general propositions. At a conference held in Chicago about five or six years ago for the purpose of discussing the legislation affecting the regulation of industrial combinations, the consideration of the Sherman Anti-Trust Law and how an amendment might be obtained, I was a member of the Committee on Resolutions. . . .

I have no apologies to make for anything that may have been said in regard to the personnel of any one connected with the National Civic Federation, but I ask you if an association such as that can agree upon such declarations to free the organizations of labor from an unjust position in which they are placed, due to the interpretation placed upon the Sherman Anti-Trust Law by the Supreme Court of the United States, is not that effort worth the making?

And I ought to say parenthetically that whenever I am at one of those dinners given by the National Civic Federation one of the things I consistently do is to abstain from eating or drinking. And I do that because I am usually called upon to speak, and I do not care to speak with my make-up full of food. But suppose we all ate heartily and suppose we all enjoyed it thoroughly? What then? Are our friends the Socialists to take umbrage at that? Reference has been made to the fact that we have eaten dinners, and "glorious dinners," while some of the working men have gone hungry. I think that if that logic were pursued we ought to fast until all of us have gotten enough to eat! I know we are all affected, some more some less, as our sentiment, our humanity, is touched by the misery or the poverty of men; but why should we go to a theatre and hear and see the performers to make us laugh and be merry while there are others in the land who shed tears of hunger and misery? I think it might be not at all remiss if we were consistent as well as sophistical.

But I have something to which I desire to call your attention. With the close of the Socialist International Congress at Copenhagen last year this appears in one of the Socialist organs, Jaures' [4] paper, of France, *L'Humanite*.

At the conclusion, however, all shook hands and held a great reception. In short, it was a congress of compromise which ended in a dance. Mr. Bourdeau thinks there was something droll in the sumptuousness of the supper given by the delegates at the magnificent town hall of Copenhagen. He says the German paper Vorwaerts described "the Pantagruelio sideboard," on which figured "hams and scarlet lobsters, and various choice dainties and delicacies which stood among long-necked bottles." "We saw nothing of the cabbage soup which Proudhon served out to his guests." *L'Humanite* (Paris) protests against such luxury. "To tell the truth," cries Mr. Jaures in his paper, after sharing the good things of the Pantagruelio sideboard, "I was ashamed to indulge in all this fine fare." The innocent orgy, says this writer, concluded with a dance. To quote his words:

"To the voluptuous measures of Viennese waltzes the couples joined arms and hands; round and round they whirled, and the god cupid was one of the party. The congress ended in delight, for the most celebrated Socialists were to be seen and admired circling in the most frantic of farandoles. A fine comment on Bernstein's[5] dictum, 'congresses are all humbug.' "

[4] Jean Juares, radical French Socialist, assassinated in 1914 for opposition to World War I.—Ed.

[5] Edward Bernstein, German radical, author of *Evolutionary Socialism*, favoring parliamentary gradualism as opposed to revolutionary class conflict to achieve socialism.—Ed.

No do we need to go to Copenhagen to find the representatives of the Socialists dining or lunching with the hated *Bourgeoise*. A few weeks ago our famous "swing-around-the-circle" President happened to go to Milwaukee, and there a luncheon was given by the manufacturers and large business men of the city. At the table occupied by the President of the United States, his military aides, and big business men (surrounded by secret service detectives) were seated the irreconcilable Socialist Mayor of Milwaukee and the redoubtable Socialist Congressman, Victor Berger. And they sat there at that table listening to the President of the United States make an attack upon the trade union position and the labor movement! And they had that as a dessert for their lunch!

When Delegate Mitchell this morning read a list of the civic bodies of which he is a member and to which he is giving service, it reminded me that I ought to just tax my memory a bit, and with the assistance of my secretary I wrote this list of the organization to which I belong: National Conference of Charities and Corrections; Committee of One Hundred on National Health; National Child Labor Committee; American Association for Labor Legislation; Roosevelt Foundation for the Promotion of Industrial Peace; The Civic Forum; The People's Institute of New York; The Society for Industrial Peace; The National Conservation Congress; The National Society for the Promotion of Industrial Education; The American Academy of Social and Political Science; The National Geographic Society; The New York State Commission to Investigate the Factory Conditions as They Exist in the State; The Society for the Prevention of Tuberculosis; the Lincoln University Endowment Society; Friends of Russian Freedom; Good Roads Congress; The Peace Society of New York; The Washington Peace Society.

Besides, I am a member of the Odd Fellows, an Elk, a Mason—I am not eligible as a member of the Knights of Columbus—but I think you will realize that I am rather a well organized man. I do not refer in this list to my primary membership, the one to which I owe my first loyalty, the Cigar Makers' International Union, my trade union.

8
The Negro Worker[1]

With few exceptions, the American worker of Gompers' time shared the anti-Negro bias of the age. Blacks were denied entrance into most craft unions, were excluded from apprentice training programs, and, when unionized at all, were segregated into all-black locals. In 1902 the distinguished Negro sociologist, W. E. B. DuBois published The Negro Artisan, *a study in which he estimated there were about 40,000 black union members, half of these in the industrially organized United Mine Workers.*

Gompers was more than a prejudiced observer; he was a bigot. White workers were, he said, "Caucasians"; but he taunted Negros, in the Federationist *and in his speeches, with the common, demeaning epithets of the day. Negro strikebreakers, a frequent employer device, were threatened by Gompers with "a race hatred far worse than any ever known." When DuBois wrote Gompers about the sad condition of black workers and enclosed a copy of* The Negro Artisan, *Gompers dismissed the study as being "neither fair nor accurate" and told DuBois that he had "more important work to attend to than correct copy for your paper."*

Black radicals were caught in a peculiar dilemma. In theory they favored the cause of the workers. But even their journals carried the label of the International Typographical Union, an AFL affiliate which, DuBois wrote in 1918, "systematically and deliberately excludes every Negro that it dares from membership, no matter what his qualifications."

Gompers' attitude toward black workers was a symptom of his racial bias. He continually favored restrictive immigration legislation and he joined with some of the more virulent race baiters of the day in questioning the humanity of any other than white men.

In his autobiography, Gompers pleads for the right of equal opportunity for "colored workmen" but he adds: "Of course, I

[1] From *AFL History, Encyclopedia, and Reference Book* (Washington, D. C., 1924), pp. 300–301.

never entertained the thought of anything approaching social equality." The selections below are drawn from the official AFL record on race relations up to 1924, original spelling retained.

(1890) A. F. of L. looks with disfavor upon trade unions having provisions in their constitutions excluding from membership persons on account of race and color and request they be expunged.

(1897) Condemned charge that unions would not admit negroes and declared: That the A. F. of L. reaffirms its declaration that it welcomes to its ranks all labor, without regard to creed, color, sex, race, or nationality, and that its best efforts have been, and will continue to be, to encourage the organization of those most needing its protection, whether they be in the North or the South, the East or the West, white or black.

(1898) This telegram was read: "Atlanta Federation of Trades declined to enter Peace Jubilee parade because negro delegates were excluded. Color line not drawn in labor organizations in South."

(1900) Endorsed plan to organize negroes in separate unions and called upon central bodies to admit them to membership.

(1901) Convention approved issuing charter to central body at Danville, Va., composed of negro workmen.

(1910) The press having misrepresented a statement made by the president of the A. F. of L. in which he was quoted as "reading the negro out of the labor movement," he said: "In reviewing the organized labor movement abroad and in the United States I called attention to the conditions confronting the working people of our time and incidentally among several things to which I referred I called attention to the fact that we had with us a population of eight million negroes, and that they are but a little more than half a century from a condition of slavery, and as a consequence it could not be expected that, as a rule, they would have the same conception of their rights and duties as other men of labor have in America. Instead of 'reading the negro out of the labor movement' my contention and the contention of the American Federation of Labor is to try to bring them into the organized labor movement of our country. We are trying our level best, and will continue to do so, to organize the men and women of toil without regard to their religion, their politics, their nationality, their sex or their race. I could not permit this entire day to pass by without thus publicly, in this convention and in the presence of our visitors and the representatives of the press, making this correction." The convention also denounced the misrepresentation, declaring: "So far from closing the doors of the organized labor movement against any wage-earner, no matter of what creed, of what color, of what nationality, of what calling, of which sex, the American Federation of Labor annually exerts its efforts and spends large sums of money in spreading the gospel of trade unionism among all who toil in the endeavor to bring them within the beneficent fold of the trade union movement every toiler of every trade and calling without respect to color or sex, religion or nationality. Reference to the report of our secretary from year to year, showing the amounts spent annually in organization work will confirm us in this statement. The conventions of the American Federation of Labor have repeatedly declared for the organization of all wage-earners without regard to class, race, creed, religion, sex or politics. This declaration is embodied in some of the literature which is kept constantly on hand at our headquarters and which is widely distributed from year to year. Separate charters may be issued to Central Labor Unions, Local Unions, or Federal Local Unions, composed exclusively of colored members, where, in the judgment of the Executive Council it appears advisable and to the best interest of the Trade Union Movement to do so. The A. F. of L., in its effort to organize all the toilers of our country so as to protect and advance their rights and interests, knows no race, no color, no creed, no nationality, no political party."

(1917) Executive Council instructed to aid Negroes in organizing.

(1918) Representatives of the negro race presented this plan of organization: President of A. F. of L. to write a letter for publication in the negro press expressing the relationship between the white and colored worker; explaining why certain internationals draw the color line and recommending its withdrawal; selection of a qualified negro for organizer and a plan of cooperation to organize these workers. The convention expressed pleasure that the leaders of the colored race realized the necessity of organizing the workers into unions affiliated with the A. F. of L. Special attention was requested in the future to the work or organization.

9

Against Socialism

Gompers lived at a time when the founders of modern socialism, Marx and Engels, set down precise formulas and prophecies on the future of industrial society. Through the accident of history, Gompers survived both men and their prophecies and he lived to reject the arguments of their disciples, the American socialists. Early in his career Gompers accused the socialists of misinterpreting Marxism and once, in the heat of a factional dispute, he appealed to Engels for support. Later, as the AFL grew, Gompers charged the socialists with the crime of Marxism and he deftly threw at them the unfulfilled prophecies and formulas which, at one time, had stirred him into class action.

The socialists knew that their credentials as working-class spokesmen were somewhat vague if they could not lead the AFL, the largest union organization of the day. Their challenges to Gompers were repeated and bitter and invariably futile. But they knew how to embarrass him. By accepting the private ownership of property—the means of production and distribution—Gompers indirectly supported the capitalist system. Gompers in turn charged the socialists with dual unionism, splitting the only real forces of working-class protection.

But as his Marxism left him and as the day-to-day struggle of union management concerned him, Gompers began to see worker–capitalist relations in a different way. The ownership of property was not important: it was the conditions of labor and the material gains of workers which were dominant. If socialism ever triumphed over capitalism, unions would continue to exist, to bargain, to strike if necessary, and to sign contracts stating the conditions of labor. Still, under capitalism or socialism, the workers would continually demand "more." When the Bolsheviks seized power, Gompers became an almost immediate enemy of the regime after he was informed that Russian trade unions were not free to strike or to bargain with the socialist commissars who replaced the capitalist managers.

The first essay ("Against Socialism") below is a composite of Gompers' thought on socialism and socialists in his years as head of the AFL. The second is an excerpt from the famous Morris

Hillquit–Samuel Gompers mutual cross-examination before the 1914 Industrial Commission. Hillquit, a leading Socialist party lawyer, and a member of the AFL, was a familiar Gompers adversary.

AGAINST SOCIALISM [1]

All the indictments made against the revolutionizing influence of machinery, the influence of trusts, the misuse of injunctions and military power have been again and again endorsed by all trade unionists, but the difference between us is one as to practice and methods. It is said the trade union movement is stagnant; that wages have been reduced and no progress has been made for years. In 1878 we had only nine national unions, and now we have sixty-eight. We have never made it a test of membership in the A. F. of L., or in any trade union, that a member should belong to any particular political party or endorse any economic creed. To do so now at this Convention would be to break faith with our members. It is charged here, because we favored free silver, we have taken political action and tied ourselves to the Democratic party. That is not true, for we endorsed free silver in 1893, three years before the Democratic party adopted it in its national platform. Because some of us stand firmly by the historical unitary and cohesive character of the trade union movement, as heretofore expounded by the A. F. of L., we are called "pure and simple." Better any time a pure and simple trade unionist than an impure and complex confusionist. Let us put an end to this continual political spirit-rapping, guided, as it is, by theoretical, speculative extremists. It is time we notified the men of isms and schisms in a labor movement that the trade union can never be sidetracked or befogged by economic theories or debatable small-potato politics. In this country let us use all political parties. Place them on record and show our people their shortcomings when they do not meet our demands. Elect trade unionists to every office and advance them on every possible occasion. Divest ourselves of petty jealousies. Arouse cohesive class feeling among the workers by industrial conflicts when forced upon us by unfair employers. Make the industrial struggle more intense so that the ties of unionism will grow stronger. This question of politics is one which involves the enmity and the integrity of the labor movement. Either the trade union movement is right or it is wrong, and the trade unionists must declare for trade unionism, without frills or feathers, or it is a confession that we are wrong. I contend

[1] From "Socialism," in *AFL History, Encyclopedia, and Reference Book* (Washington, D. C., 1924).

that the trade union movement is the history of the development of the labor movement—of the expression, aye, the crystallized expression of discontent of the workers. "By their deeds shall ye know them," rather than by their honeyed and smooth words, with which they seek to allure our movement into such a vortex of complications and capture our movement as a tail to their political party kite. If they were to express themselves in this Convention as they do outside of it they would not be tolerated in the Convention two minutes, and I propose to succinctly call attention to the difference between the mask and the real face of the Socialists who advocate and have presented the proposition contained in the amendment to this resolution now before the house, and which embodies the idea which would disrupt this organization. They have done all they could to mistreat the organization and wage-earners in the trade unions, and to disrupt them. Aye, one of the parties referred to called a convention for the purpose of forming a rival to the A. F. of L.—a rival to the trade unionist movement, a rival to the economic movement, and at the convention they had upon the broad streamer decorating the chairman's stand, emblazoned in colors of red: "Wreck the Old Trade Unions; Pull for the Shore of Socialism." They have besmirched the name of Labor and sought to destroy our organization; they have attacked the honor, fidelity and manliness and the principles of the men who have tried to stand by the workers in their natural struggle for bettering the conditions of today. The men who did not grope, but have fought in the struggle and have never shirked their duty nor their responsibilities, the trade unionists, have met the problems as they arise, and are willing, not simply to indulge in what is known as radical resolutions or radical talk, but enter right into the midst of the battle and take the responsibilities, no matter what the result might be to them.

As a matter of fact, the trade union form of organization is the historic and natural form of associated effort of the working people. The nearer and closer we hew to the line of trade unionism, exercising the functions as trade unions, the more direct and successful will be the progress of our movement. I heard a delegate on the floor of the convention say, that if you elected six Socialist Congressmen in the U. S., you will have very many changes. I respectfully call the delegate's attention to the fact that in the German Parliament there are nearly 100 Socialists, and there we find the most backward of all European countries in the interest of labor. The man who is held up to typify Socialism is [K]arl Marx. There is not a socialist that can find in all his utterances one word for a co-operative commonwealth. During his life, he wrote not only his work, "Das Kapital," but he wrote a number of other works, and in one of them, replying to

Prou[d]hon, he denounced the socialists as the worst enemies of the laboring classes. I know that the socialists have taken that pamphlet and made a foot-note on it, and said that [K]arl Marx, in writing that, did not have the socialists of today in mind, but I call the attention of the gentleman who made that foot-note that it was made when [K]arl Marx was dead, not when he was alive, when he would have had an opportunity of repudiating those who wanted to expurgate the statement that he made.

Attention has been called to the conduct of the men who clothed themselves in the mantle of Socialism, and assumed a position of superiority, mentally, in honesty, in work, and in ennobling purposes. It is because their professions are in entire discord with their actions in this Convention that it is necessary to call their position in question. I shall not refer at this time to their very many detailed acts of treachery to the trade union movement; but I shall refer to some of the declarations made upon the floor of the Convention by delegates participating in this discussion, and show you that though they may believe themselves to be trade unionists, they are at heart, and logically, the antagonists of our movement. Our friends, the Socialists, always when with us have an excellent conception of the trouble in our industrial life. They say, as we say, and as every intelligent man or woman says, that there are miseries which surround us. We recognize the poverty, we know the sweatshop, we can play on every string of the harp, and touch the tenderest chords of human sympathy; but while we recognize the evil and would apply the remedy, our Socialist friends would look forward to the promised land, and wait for "the sweet by-and-by." Their statements as to economic ills are right: their conclusions and their philosophy are all askew. The action of the committee has been found fault with because they did not bring in a substitute for the resolutions presented, but instead took a course that will bring this matter fairly and squarely before the Convention. At the last Convention in New Orleans, through placing us in a false position, the resolution upon this question came within an ace of being adopted; but this year the committee has made this question a plain, broad proposition. The vote that will be recorded here today against the report of the committee will be fairly and squarely recorded in favor of Socialism; and the vote that is recorded in favor of the committee's report will be against Socialism. And it will be recognized as such throughout the land. There has not been a legislative body before which the other officers of the Federation or I myself have appeared, nor an association of employers, nor individual employers with whom we have met in conference but that we have been confronted with this Socialist amendment, so-called, which came near being passed at New Orleans. It has made, and will make, our work doubly difficult, because these employers have refused and do refuse to confer for the adjustment of difficulties and disputes when they are led to believe by declaration that property is in danger of confiscation. We have been asked how many trade unionists there are in Congress. I venture to say that there are more trade unionists in Congress and in our state legislatures holding clear cards than there are elsewhere in similar positions the world over. Do you suppose the Socialists want trade unionists elected to Congress and to the legislatures? [Delegate: "No"] Of course, no. Of course, Socialist delegates, no. I am proud of you for your honesty in admitting it. But what he has admitted on the floor is true of every other Socialist in the Convention. As a matter of fact, wherever there has been a trade unionist candidate for any political office, if there have been half a dozen Socialists in town, they have always tried to defeat the trade unionists. Now, there has been a remark made about the passage of the military law by Congress. I agree it would have been a good thing if we could have prevented the passage of that law, but the delegate said that if we even had a minority in Congress, it could not have become law. I point him to the fact that in Germany they have the largest number of any party in the parliament of that country, and yet they have the most tyrannical military laws of any country on the globe. It is all very well to make a declaration, but the facts are another thing. We are told we ought not to rely upon an indiscreet remark by a Socialist here and there; but if not, then why rely upon the remarks of trade unionists here and there? Yes, an indiscreet remark—but the difficulty here and outside of the Conventions of the A. F. of L. is to find a Socialist who is not all the time guilty of making indiscreet remarks. He is at it all the time. When the Socialist Trade and Labor Alliance broke away because of the domination of one man they started out to form a new socialist party and declared what one delegate announced on the floor of this Convention— the trade unionists must be unhampered and fought from within. One of the reasons I am not with the Socialist party is because I want to be in line with the declaration that the trade union policy, the movement and the work, must be unhampered by your political nostrums. When the Socialists formed the American Labor Union in rivalry to the A. F. of L. I took occasion to continually say in the American Federationist that it was but another attempt to form another Socialist Trade and Labor Alliance, without its practical courage to openly declare its enmity to the American trade union movement. Is it not a fact that no matter what we achieve, we are belittled by the Socialists? Even the Labor Day we have achieved for all the people of our country—the proposition comes in here to abolish it and to make Labor Day in line with the Labor Day of continental Europe, May 1st.

Men of labor, if you were in the office of the A. F. of L. for a time and you knew the things that transpire in the labor movement in a general and in a specific way—for they are all focussed there, and we know what is going on and we know the enemies of the labor movement—you would have your opinion clear cut upon this subject. Why, we have spent more money in organizing in Colorado itself than in any other state, notwithstanding that, industrially considered, it ought to cost very little. I want to tell you, Socialists, that I have studied your philosophy; read your works upon economics, and not the meanest of them; studied your standards works, both in English and German—have not only read, but studied them. I have heard your orators and watched the work of your movement the world over. I have kept close watch upon your doctrines for thirty years; have been closely associated with many of you, and know how you think and what you propose. I know, too, what you have up your sleeve. And I want to say that I am entirely at variance with your philosophy. I declare to you, I am not only at variance with your doctrines, but with your philosophy. Economically, you are unsound; socially, you are wrong; industrially, you are an impossibility.

NO ULTIMATE END [2]

Mr. Hillquit: Now, . . . is it your conception, Mr. Gompers, or that of the Federation, that workers in the United States today receive the full product of their labor?

Mr. Gompers: I think, but I am not quite so sure, that I know what you have in mind.

Mr. Hillquit: Do you understand my question?

Mr. Gompers: I think I do, but in the generally accepted sense of that term, no.

Mr. Hillquit: In any particular sense, yes?

Mr. Gompers: No.

Mr. Hillquit: Then the workers of this country do not receive the whole product of their labor? Can you hazard a guess as to what proportion of the product they do receive in the shape of wages? . . .

[2] From testimony of May 22, 1914, U. S. Congress, Senate, *Final Report and Testimony,* submitted to Congress by the Commission on Industrial Relations, 64th Congress, 1st Session, Senate Document 415 (Washington: U. S. Government Printing Office, 1916), II, 1526–29.

Mr. Gompers: I will say that it is impossible for anyone to definitely say what proportion the workers receive as the result of their labor; but it is the fact that due to the organized-labor movement they have received and are receiving a larger share of the product of their labor than they ever did in the history of modern society.

Mr. Hillquit: Then one of the functions of organized labor is to increase the share of the workers in the product of their labor, is that correct?

Mr. Gompers: Yes, sir; organized labor makes constantly increasing demands upon society for reward for the services which the workers give to society, and without which the civilized life would be impossible.

Mr. Hillquit: And these demands for an increasing share of the reward of the product of labor continue by a gradual process all the time?

Mr. Gompers: I am not so sure as to gradual process. Sometimes it is not a gradual process, but it is all the time.

Mr. Hillquit: All the time?

Mr. Gompers: Yes, sir.

Mr. Hillquit: Then, Mr. Gompers, you assume that the organized labor movement has generally succeeded in forcing a certain increase of that portion of the workers in the share of the general product, do you?

Mr. Gompers: Yes, sir.

Mr. Hillquit: And it demands more now?

Mr. Gompers: Yes, sir.

Mr. Hillquit: And if it should get, say, 5 per cent more within the next year, will the organized labor movement rest contented with that and stop?

Mr. Gompers: Not if I know anything about human nature.

Mr. Hillquit: Will the organized labor movement, or the labor movement of the country generally, stop in its demands for an ever greater share in the product at any time before it has received or does receive the full product, and before in its eyes complete social justice shall have been done?

Mr. Gompers: That question again that you have bobbed up with quite serenely in regard to the share of the product of labor, say that the working people—and I prefer to say working pepole and speak of them as real human beings—the working people, as all other people, they are prompted by the same desires and hopes of a better life, and they are not willing to wait until after they have shuffled off this mortal coil for the better life, they want it here and now, and they want to make conditions better for their children so that they may meet the other, the newer problems in their time. The working people are pressing forward, pressing forward, making their claims and presenting those claims with whatever power they have, to exercise it in a normal, rational manner, to secure a larger, and constantly larger share of the products. They are working to the highest and best ideals of social justice.

Mr. Hillquit: Now, the highest and best ideals of social justice, as applied to the distribution of wealth, wouldn't that be a system under which the workers, manual, mental, directive, executive and all other lines together get the sum total of all the products we supply them?

Mr. Gompers: Really, a fish is caught by the tempting bait: a mouse or a rat is caught in a trap by the tempting bait; the intelligent, comprehensive, common-sense workmen prefer to deal with the problems of today, the problem which confronts them today, with which they are bound to contend if they want to advance, rather than to deal with a picture and a dream which has never had, and I am sure never will have, any reality in the affairs of humanity, and which threaten, if it could be introduced, the worst system of circumscriptional effort and activity that has ever been invented by the ken of the human kind.

Mr. Hillquit: That is what I want to get from you, Mr. Gompers, but I would like to get an answer. In your experience with the labor movement and in its ever forward march toward greater and greater improvement, and a greater and greater share of social justice, can you point out any line where the labor movement will stop and rest contented so long as it may receive short of the full product of its work?

Mr. Gompers: I say that the workers, as human beings, will never stop in any effort, nor stop at any point in the effort to secure greater improvements in their condition, a better life in all its phases. And wherever that may lead, whatever that may be, so far in my time and my age I decline to permit my mind or my activities to be labeled by any particular ism. . . .

Mr. Hillquit: In your political work of the labor movement is the American Federation of Labor guided by a general social philosophy, or is it not?

Mr. Gompers: It is guided by the history of the past, drawing its lessons from history, to know of the conditions by which the working people are surrounded and confronted; to work along the lines of least resistance; to accomplish the best results in improving the condition of the working people, men and women and children, today and tomorrow and tomorrow—and tomorrow's tomorrow; and each day making it a better day than the one that had gone before. That is the guiding principle and philosophy and aim of the labor movement—in order to secure a better life for all.

Mr. Hillquit: But in these efforts to improve conditions from day to day you must have an underlying standard of what is better, don't you?

Mr. Gompers: No. You start out with a given program, and everything must conform to it; and if the facts do not conform to your theories, why, your declarations, or, rather, your actions, betray the state of mind "so much the worse for the facts."

Mr. Hillquit: Mr. Gompers, what I ask you is this: You say you try to make the conditions of the workers better every day. In order to determine whether the conditions are better or worse you must have some standards by which you distinguish the bad from the good in the labor movement, do you not?

Mr. Gompers: Certainly. Well, is that—

Mr. Hillquit (interrupting): Now, just—

Mr. Gompers (interrupting): Well, one moment. Does it require much discernment to know that a wage of $3 a day and a workday of 8 hours a day in sanitary workshops are all better than $2.50 a day and 12 hours a day and under perilous conditions of labor? It does not require much conception of a social philosophy to understand that.

Mr. Hillquit: Then, Mr. Gompers, by the same parity of reasoning, $4 a day and seven hours a day of work and very attractive working conditions are still better?

Mr. Gompers: Unquestionably.

Mr. Hillquit: Therefore—

Mr. Gompers (interrupting): Just a moment. I have not stipulated $4 a day or $8 a day or any number of dollars a day or eight hours a day or seven hours a day or any number of hours a day, but the best possible conditions obtainable for the workers is the aim.

Mr. Hillquit: Yes; and when these conditions are obtained—

Mr. Gompers (interrupting): Why, then, we want better.

Mr. Hillquit (continuing): You will still strive for better?

Mr. Gompers: Yes.

Mr. Hillquit: Now, my question is, Will this effort on the part of organized labor ever stop until it has the full reward for its labor?

Mr. Gompers: It won't stop at all.

Mr. Hillquit: That is a question—

Mr. Gompers (interrupting): Not when any particular point is reached, whether it be that toward which you have just declared or anything else. The working people will never stop—

Mr. Hillquit: Exactly.

Mr. Gompers (continuing): In their effort to obtain a better life for themselves and for their wives and for their children and for humanity.

Mr. Hillquit: Then, the object of the labor union is to obtain complete social justice for themselves and for their wives and for their children?

Mr. Gompers: It is the effort to obtain a better life every day.

Mr. Hillquit: Every day and always—

Mr. Gompers: Every day. That does not limit it.

Mr. Hillquit: Until such time—

Mr. Gompers: Not until any time.

Mr. Hillquit: In other words—

Mr. Gompers (interrupting): In other words, we go further than you. (Laughter and applause in the audience.) You have an end; we have not. . . .

Mr. Gompers: . . . Under Socialism will there be liberty of individual action, and liberty in the choice of occupation and refusal to work?

Mr. Hillquit: Plenty of it, Mr. Gompers.

Mr. Gompers: I take it that you have no apprehension that under a democratic Socialist management, the administrators could or would attempt to exploit the workers under them, and one set of laborers would exploit another set; the lazy office-holders, the industrious artisans; the strong and bolder, the weaker and more modest ones, and the failures, the economically successful.

Mr. Hillquit: I think it quite likely that there will be some abuses of that kind. Even under Socialism men will still remain human, no doubt. But, Mr. Gompers, we have every reason to believe that they will be small and insignificant as compared with present abuses, for the system will be based on a greater democracy and self-government, and will thus provide for proper means of remedy. Furthermore, there will be no great incentive to corruption such as we have in private gain under capitalism.

Mr. Gompers: In the event that the Co-operative Commonwealth should be established, taking it for granted for the sake of the question, that it is possible, it would have for its present purpose the highest material and social and moral improvement of the condition of the workers attainable at that time, would it not?

Mr. Hillquit: I think so.

Mr. Gompers: And would there be any higher aim after that is established?

Mr. Hillquit: Oh, there will be plenty more. There will be new aims coming every day.

Mr. Gompers: Still more?

Mr. Hillquit: Still further.

Mr. Gompers: Still higher?

Mr. Hillquit: Still higher.

Mr. Gompers: Now, if that is so, isn't it a fact that it is not at all a goal, but simply a transitory ideal?

Mr. Hillquit: Sure. It is our goal to-day. It is a transitory goal. There will be a movement toward a higher goal to-morrow.

Mr. Gompers: In other words, you think even if that condition of affairs should be possible, it, like the conditions of to-day, is transitory and continually tending toward improvement?

Mr. Hillquit: Yes.

Mr. Gompers: And not a goal?

Mr. Hillquit: Not an ultimate goal. There is no such thing as an ultimate social goal.

Mr. Gompers: In the Socialist state, would you have each worker rewarded by the full product of his labor, or by an apportionment of the product according to his demands? In other words, would the rule be, to each according to his deeds, or to each according to his needs?

Mr. Hillquit: I think neither, strictly speaking. I don't suppose his Socialist regime would at once radically change established standards of compensation. I think it would have to grow up and be built up on the existing basis. And I think it will largely be a system of salaries and wages, as nearly as possible, in proportion to the usefulness of the service—but they will be larger than they are to-day, because they will include the profits now paid to the idle capitalists.

Mr. Gompers: So, as a matter of fact, then, if the Co-operative Commonwealth is not a goal, is not an end, then why term it Socialism, and why not term it the ordinary, natural development of the human race to a higher and better state of society?

Mr. Hillquit: We may term it the ordinary and natural development of the human race to the point of Socialism. In other words, Mr. Gompers, we divide the history of mankind pretty arbitrarily into certain periods. We speak of the period of Slavery, the period of

Feudalism, the period of Capitalism. Now we foresee the next step in development, and call it the period of Socialism. We cannot draw a line of demarcation where it starts or where it vanishes. It will certainly not be permanent. There will be something superior to it some time. In the meantime every stage of development is superior to the preceding stage; and by the same token as Capitalism is superior to Feudalism, Socialism is superior to Capitalism. That is all.

Mr. Gompers: You simply apply it as a term, and not an end?

Mr. Hillquit: Not an ultimate end in social development, no.

10

All that Is Unlawful Is Not Criminal[1]

Gompers testified before Congress in 1904 in favor of an anti-injunction bill which would modify the "conspiracy" and "coercion" principles of the common law and the Sherman Antitrust Act. The reform measure failed to pass, and injunctions were used increasingly to stop strikes. The extract which follows is from Gompers' most succinct attack on legal opposition to union power.

There are times when we have tried to have injunctions modified; in some instances our requests were granted, but very few. As a rule the hearings were set for so long a time after the issuance of injunctions that we have always accepted it that that was the first time we had an opportunity of being heard in the matter at all. Then, as I have said in the opening of my remarks, the thing upon which these injunctions might be modified would be the exercise of those rights which we have the perfect lawful right to exercise, and the things which would not be modified are already covered by existing laws, for they are alleged crimes.

I say as a layman, but with the conscientiousness of the responsibility which goes with it, that there is not a man who will assert that there is one law upon the statute books of the United States upon which these injunctions are based. You can not quote a law which gives the authority for the issuance of these injunctions in these disputes. One gentleman drew the fine line between what is unlawful and what is a crime. Truly, all that is a crime is unlawful; all that is unlawful is not criminal. But the alleged charges upon which these injunctions are based are crimes, alleged crimes, and the others are neither crimes nor are they unlawful.

We have been told that the bill if enacted would be unconstitutional. Well, that has been the last cry of the opposition about every reform bill that has ever been passed by Congress. Now, if the gentle-

[1] From *Textbook of Labor's Political Demands* (Washington, D. C., 1906).

men who oppose this bill believe that it would be unconstitutional, why exercise themselves so much about it?

Our opponents, of course, agree that it is lawful to strike, to strike as an individual or collectively. It is perfectly lawful, perfectly lawful now. It was not always lawful, and the predecessors of the gentlemen who now oppose this bill occupied exactly the same position that they now do when we sought the modification of the laws of conspiracy, so far as they apply to strikes, the right to strike, to quit work, to seek a new employer, to seek better conditions. It is not so long ago when it was a conspiracy to strike; it was not so long ago when it was unlawful.

I think it almost superfluous to say that the charge that the leaders of organized labor either teach or encourage the commission of violence or crime is a base fabrication and unworthy even of the gentlemen who oppose this bill. The men who form largely the employers of labor of the country know that that is not true, and the gentlemen who have given vent to that utterance know in their heart of hearts that that is not true, and that the men who are so-called leaders of labor either in their respective trades or in the general labor movement have done and are doing their best to prevent any violence of any sort, either by an individual man or by any number of them, union or nonunion.

The insinuation that the labor leaders do not represent the rank and file of the organized workmen is upon its surface simply a preposterous statement. One of the gentlemen said he represents the workmen of the country. Yes, I think he does; very much like the lion represented the lamb after he had eaten him.

We are fully persuaded that this bill is for the right. It is for justice, it is in the interest of right and in the interest of justice. It is in the line of the evolutionary progress of the social development and the economic development of our country.

The American organized workmen realize the conditions by which they are surrounded and confronted. They understand the great concentrations of industry and combinations of wealth. They have realized the fact that individually they have no opportunity either to defend their own rights, to redress a grievance, or to attain an improvement in their condition.

They understand that if they expect amelioration to-day or to-morrow and for the time to come, to preserve their manhood and integrity and independence and sovereignty, they must organize and unite and federate. I know that there are some men who answer that the organized labor movement, with its three million members (I am including those who are not directly affiliated with the American Federation of Labor), do not represent the majority of the laborers of the country. I agree that we do not represent a majority of the workingmen of our country. But I venture to say that we represent the most intelligent and the most skillful and the most manly of the workingmen of our country, and this, too, without any reflection upon any nonunion man.

That there is a legal remedy for some of the things which an injunction can enjoin, goes without saying; but it is the purpose of the opponents of our legislation on this subject to get rid of the trial by jury in the regular process of the law. Their purpose is to make the judge who issues the injunction, the judge, the jury and executioner, and indeed to take away from the workmen enjoined the constitutional right of being tried before a jury of their peers for any crime or offense with which they may be charged.

Gentlemen of the committee, labor asks for nothing but what she believes she is entitled to, and organized labor is simply expressing it, because we have intelligence enough to organize and discuss these things, and out of it all has come a unanimity of judgment that this bill is necessary to the interests of peace and good will and success and progress.

I trust, in fact I have no hesitancy in believing, that the committee will report this bill favorably to the House, and that it may pass with an overwhelming vote before the adjournment of the Congress, and may become part of the laws of our land. . . .

But the doing, as I say, of the most ordinary things, that men do in their everyday lives are more and more coming to be touched upon by injunctions. One injunction was issued—or, rather, many injunctions were issued—prohibiting persuasion and not even designating what kind of persuasion. We can understand that there is such a thing as persuasion glibly used by the tongue and a club held in the hand; and no one can at all justify such persuasion as that. But even so, in such a case the injunction should not lie, because such an attempt is a threatened assault upon the person, for which there is a law to prevent, to apprehend, to try, and to convict and to punish. But there is a persuasion—that persuasion which is commonly understood in our language—which no man can deny the right to exercise by another.

And then comes the inhibition of a man or a number of men from weaning away from an employer those who are in his employ. "Weaning away!" Is there any unlawful conduct if you, in your own interest, can wean away from me a man employed by me? Weaning away from me a man who is valuable to me in my business. By what? By bribes? By payment of money? By promises of reward, by advancement, by advantage? Is not that your right? If it is your right, is it not mine?

Take a case in point. A strike occurs. Men leave the employment of a certain firm because they ask for a high wage, or protest against a cutting of their wage, and another man or men take the places made vacant by the strikers. The strikers, having had experience, have accumulated certain funds, and they approach the men who have taken their places, and say to them, "John," or "Gentlemen," or

> Men, you are taking our places. You have taken our places, and you are doing yourselves as well as us an injury, for if we are defeated in our effort the wages will be reduced and stay reduced, or our efforts to increase wages will not succeed, and you will have been the instrument to our defeat and to your own defeat and disadvantage.
>
> Come with us. Make common cause with us. We have accumulated funds, and we will pay you from what we receive from our associated efforts and our accumulated funds, either as much as you can earn, as much as we get, or we will pay you more than what you are now earning; quit the employment of that firm, and by reason of our common concert of action make that impression upon the firm that it will be required to yield and to withdraw the offer of the reduction of wages, or to concede the increase.

I hold that the workmen have the right go to any workmen employed by anybody, whether in a strike-bound establishment or otherwise, and offer this man to quit his employment and go to work with them in some other establishment, or not to work at all, for the time being. They have the right to "lure away" and "wean away" from an employer a workman, and to offer him money inducements, so that he may quit that employment and work for another, or to go idle for a period, in order that a certain lawful, honorable purpose may be achieved. And yet the injunction is issued against workmen for doing that very thing, and for doing it after the injunction has been issued they have been sent to jail.

11

Labor's Bill of Grievances: The Shift into Politics

When relief from injunctions failed to pass in Congress, the AFL, prodded by Gompers, began a campaign to defeat proinjunction Congressmen and elect organized labor's advocates. The "Bill of Grievances," published as "Labor's Textbook," was presented to members of Congress in the spring of an election year (1906), with implied threats of massive union political involvement in the fall.

LABOR'S BILL OF GRIEVANCES [1]

Eight-Hour Law

The law commonly known as the Eight-Hour Law has been found ineffective and insufficient to accomplish the purpose of its designers and framers. Labor has, since 1894, urged the passage of a law so as to remedy the defects, and for its extension to all work done for or on behalf of the government. Our efforts have been in vain.

Without hearing of any kind granted to those who are the advocates of the eight-hour law and principle, Congress passed, and the President signed, an appropriation bill containing a rider nullifying the eight-hour law and principle in its application to the greatest public work ever undertaken by our government, the construction of the Panama Canal.

The eight-hour law in terms provides that those entrusted with the supervision of government work shall neither require nor permit any violation thereof. The law has been grievously and frequently violated. The violations have been reported to the heads of several departments, who have refused to take the necessary steps for its enforcement.

Convict Labor

While recognizing the necessity for the employment of inmates of our penal institutions, so that they may be self-supporting, labor has

[1] From *Textbook of Labor's Political Demands* (Washington, D. C., 1906).

urged in vain the enactment of a law that shall safeguard it from the competition of the labor of convicts.

Immigration

In the interest of all of our people, and in consonance with their almost general demand, we have urged Congress for some tangible relief from the constantly growing evil of induced and undesirable immigration, but without result.

Chinese Exclusion

Recognizing the danger of Chinese immigration, and responsive to the demands of the people, Congress years ago enacted an effective Chinese exclusion law; yet, despite the experience of the people of our own country, as well as those of other countries, the present law is flagrantly violated, and now, by act of Congress, it is seriously proposed to invalidate that law and reverse the policy.

Seamen's Rights

The partial relief secured by the laws of 1895 and 1898, providing that seamen shall not be compelled to endure involuntary servitude, has been seriously threatened at each succeeding Congress. The petitions to secure for the seamen equal rights with all others have been denied, and a disposition shown to extend to other workmen the system of compulsory labor.

Trusts and Interstate Commerce

The anti-trust and interstate commerce laws enacted to protect the people against monopoly in the products of labor, and against discrimination in the transportation thereof, have been perverted, so far as the laborers are concerned, so as to invade and violate their personal liberty as guaranteed by the constitution. Our repeated efforts to obtain redress from Congress have been in vain.

Anti-Injuction Bill

The beneficent writ of injunction, intended to protect property rights has, as used in labor disputes, been perverted so as to attack and destroy personal freedom, and in a manner to hold that the employer has some property rights in the labor of the workmen. Instead of obtaining the relief which labor has sought, it is seriously threatened with statutory authority for existing judicial usurpation.

Right of Petition Denied Government Employees

Recently the President issued an order forbidding any and all government employes, upon the pain of instant dismissal from the government service, to petition Congress for any redress of grievances or for any improvement in their condition. Thus the constitutional right of citizens to petition must be surrendered by the government employe in order that he may obtain or retain his employment.

Redress of Grievances

We present these grievances to your attention because we have long, patiently, and in vain waited for redress. There is not any matter of which we have complained but for which we have, in an honorable and lawful manner, submitted remedies. The remedies for these grievances proposed by labor are in line with fundamental law, and with the progress and development made necessary by changed industrial conditions.

Labor brings these its grievances to your attention because you are the representatives responsible for legislation and for failure of legislation. The toilers comes to you as your fellow citizens, who, by reason of their position in life, have not only with all other citizens an equal interest in our country, but the further interest of being the burden bearers, the wage-earners of America. As labor's representatives we ask you to redress these grievances, for it is in your power so to do.

Labor now appeals to you, and we trust that it may not be in vain. But if, perchance, you may not heed us, we shall appeal to the conscience and the support of our fellow citizens.

12
NAM Plot to Bribe Gompers[1]

The attempted bribe of Gompers in 1907 was reported by him with great emotion during the AFL annual convention later that year. The socialist faction within the AFL planned to challenge the leadership for its role in the National Civic Federation, but the "bribe" revelations forced a tone of uncommon unity among all factions. (The NCF attack was delayed until 1911.) For two hours Gompers spoke of the bribe fiasco and hinted at even more sensational facts.

About a month ago, September 28, when I was leaving the Victoria Hotel, 27th Street and Broadway, 27th Street exit, New York, a man accosted me: "Hello, Mr. Gompers." I said, "Hello." We shook hands. He said, "You remember me; I was a newspaper man and met you on the platform at the immigration conference last year. My name is Brandenburg." I told him I was sure I had seen him somewhere but could not locate him, and was pleased to see him again. He said, "Mr. Gompers, I am now in the employ of the National Association of Manufacturers in their campaign against labor, and I am against you, but I have known you and known you favorably and like you, and I think you ought to get together with Mr. Van Cleave and come to a better understanding as to your contentions, and I am in a position to help." I answered that our position toward the National Association of Manufacturers was defensive; that I did not aim to attack the organization as such or Mr. Van Cleave as its president, but I was not going to permit him to make all sorts of attacks upon the labor movement without resenting them; that after all what our movement aimed to achieve was a better understanding with employers whether as individuals or associations, and, therefore I was favorable to a conciliatory policy. He said he thought an interview between Mr. Van Cleave and myself could be arranged some time. He said, however, that it would necessarily have to be between Mr. Van Cleave and myself alone. I said that we could discuss that matter some other

[1]From *Report of the Proceedings of the Twenty-eighth Annual Convention of the American Federation of Labor* (Washington, D. C., 1907), pp. 248–50.

time. About seven o'clock that same evening I returned to the hotel to get some baggage when the porter in charge of the coatroom handed me a note with the remark that the gentleman said he should hand it to me as soon as I got in and that he was waiting for me in his room. Opening the note I found it to be an unsigned request that he desired to see me upon a matter of importance and immediately in his room. I had already made other important engagements and consequently could not go to see him. [Later, a meeting was arranged with Brandenburg.]

He said:

> The purpose of my coming to see you is of the utmost importance to us. I am in charge of a certain bureau of a department organized for the National Manufacturers' Association. The purpose of it is to expose the immorality and dishonesty of the leaders in the labor movement and to make it public. We have gone into the records of every prominent man in the A. F. of L., and we have affidavits of a number of men, executive officers of national unions who implicate you and others, showing the immoral lives you and they have lived. All this is gathered and most of it is sworn statements. The time that you were ill at Little Rock, Arkansas, in 1895, the nature of your illness is known, and it was reported to us that you had, expecting to die, made a statement, being a sort of a confession. My object in coming to you is to say that I want to save you. I want you to make a statement, something that would appear as if you had written it at that time, which would in no way cast any blame upon yourself, but would show a spirit of broad kindness to others whom you desired to save, a sort of "Thanatopsis."

He handed me a paper that he had prepared. I read it twice, and realizing that he endeavored to impress upon my mind his knowledge of my supposed guilt, it was with the greatest mental concentration that I was able to contain myself. However, for the purpose of disarming any suspicion on his part that I resented his statement and for the purpose of having him go on further, I said, "Well, I do not pretend to have been an angel." I made this statement for its literal truth, he evidently accepting it as a part acquiescence in his insinuations. He then proceeded:

> As I say, I want to save you and while I do not want to express in specific financial terms what the National Association of Manufacturers is willing to do, yet I can guarantee that you will be financially safe for the balance of your life. All that you need to do is to give us the information which we want of the other men, and to give us the workings of the inner circle of your Council and the general labor movement. We do not want you to get out of the presidency of the Federation at the forthcoming convention, for the Manufacturers' As-

sociation does not like Duncan any more than they do you. They realize that if you were to get out now it would mean that he would be your successor; but in a month or two after your re-election at Norfolk, you can get out, and the publication of all of these matters in regard to the active men in the labor movement would destroy them, and they would have to get some nobody to be president and then there would be little Federation left.

The paper Brandenburg asked me to sign has never left my possession. It is as follows:

So by devious ways I have come in view of the end of the period. Not far away is the final cessation of something mortal, that I know, but that mystery of the suspension of other things immortal must yet be made clear. Soon I shall stand where I shall see with unblinded eyes, and to that point must come everyone no matter by what path, and the realization of that fact palliates the bitterness with which I could contemplate my own course were it not true. For I have struggled with the humblest on a plane of equality, and I have walked and talked with the mighty ones of the earth and have lent them my power. The poor cigarmaker's apprentice has lived to become the master of a million minds, and lived a little longer to be what he is today, not even a master of himself. There is nothing of the whine in this. Emptied, broken as I am, I have nothing to ask. Nothing I might achieve would matter in a little while, and this what I write is after all nothing more than my retrospective thoughts expressed through the accustomed medium of my pen. Wisdom is cumulative and out of my abundance I might endow posterity. Vengeance by the law of compensation over- reaches the grave, and I might undo more men a score of times than will regret my passing. Justice is exquisitely elusive and I might with a truth here and there palliate many a grave miscarriage. But why? Why should I, having driven on to my own aims leave my own disabled chariot to retrace the hippodrome? Each man in his way, be it great or small, exists in an attitude toward the world at large, in a second attitude toward his immediate associates, and in a third and almost invariably different, very different, before his own inner consciousness. Stripped of the sophistry that served as a mental lubricant when in activity, I stand at halt contemplating my own ego. I see lust of power that has triumphed again and again.

And there it abruptly stopped. I have these documents here for the inspection of any delegate who wishes to see them. There is in my possession further information of the ramifications and machinations of the National Association of Manufacturers, their detective agencies, their auxiliary companies, and the reptile hirelings who are employed to assassinate the character of the men of labor and thereby hope to weaken or destroy the labor movement of our country. All that I now desire to add is that there is not a scintilla of truth in anything published or which can be published by the National Association of Manufacturers or their hirelings which in any way can reflect upon the integrity, the morality, or the honesty of myself, and I have an abiding faith that they cannot do so of any one member of the A. F. of L. I defy our enemies to do their worst.

[At the conclusion of the statement the entire Convention arose and applauded President Gompers. A handsome basket of roses and chrysanthemums was then presented to President Gompers on behalf of the delegation from the United Hatters of North America. Editor, AFL *Proceedings,* 1907.]

Delegate Berger[2]—Mr. Chairman and fellow delegates: "For some years past it has been my lot to come here and vote against the unanimous election of President Gompers. This year I propose to move to make his election unanimous. [Applause.] I move a vote of confidence in President Gompers and the entire Executive Council. I move that everybody stand up." The motion was seconded and carried by a unanimous rising vote, accompanied by three cheers for President Gompers.

[2] [Victor Berger, Milwaukee socialist opponent of Gompers.]

13

McNamara Case Mea Culpa[1]

The McNamara brothers confessed to the Los Angeles Times bomb plot after Gompers rushed to their defense. The national press suggested that the case revealed a fanaticism and desperation in high union circles, suggesting that Gompers and his cohorts be purged.

We have nothing to hide. We are ready at any time for the agents of the law to begin investigating. Files, records of all kinds, account books—everything in documentary shape is open to them. All that has been printed, or spoken, or written to our correspondents is subject to their inquiries. Every act of every official may be freely looked into. No one is going to dodge or run away. Whatever can be done to aid the law will be done at these offices.

This is our reply at headquarters of the American Federation of Labor to the clamor to get at "the men higher up," to the repeated announcements in the press of "a nation-wide investigation by Federal officials," to the assertions that behind the McNamaras were men standing high in the councils of labor.

As to the future, how is trade unionism to be affected? With respect to this question we have looked for light from the press and in the letters coming to us in quantities from all parts of the country. What lessons are to be derived from this case, which is one of abnormalities? What illuminating suggestion has been sent in, by friend or enemy? Is organized labor to depart from its regularly adopted policies; and if so, why? Where lies a better course than that which it has followed?

Nothing new has come, in reply to these queries. Among the intense participants in the social conflict, the same groups are but reiterating their well-known sentiments. What could be expected from the National Manufacturing Association, their agents and hirelings, but precisely what they are saying—which is merely what they have been saying? What from the Socialists except to employ the occasion for vote-catching? What from such reactionary organs as the New York

[1] From *Report of the Proceedings of the Thirty-Second Annual Convention of the American Federation of Labor* (Washington, D. C., 1912), pp. 145–47.

Sun but diatribes covering half the editorial page? So long as these declared enemies of the trade unions are what they are, and unionism is what it is, no help can come from them to the labor movement.

From the social elements that stand somewhat apart from the wage conflict, there have usually come merely the suggestions of partly informed observers. Ought our Federation at once change its officials? Some part of the daily press, seeking to create a popular cry, calls for this move. That is worth no attention. Ought our Federation forthwith change its policies? The question in reply must be, Which of them? Each represents the wisdom derived from experience.

A few humanitarians are declaring that a unionism must prevail which is grounded on "industrial liberty." It will have to be a new unionism with new unionists—and where are they to be found?—for the deceits in the catchwords "industrial liberty" are known to all wageworkers who have suffered from the unending competition which is an inseparable feature of a so-called "free labor market."

As to the critics of our Federation's officers, most of them move in a fundamental error. They assume that the separate trade unions, in their organization, work and affairs, are controlled, directed, supervised from our Washington center. This is not in the least so. To the national (or international) unions there is nothing "higher up." With respect to their routine procedures, their conventions, and their dues, assessments, benefits, not one of them is subject to orders from the Federation offices. They are autonomous. All of them are in the Federation under certain general regulations, chiefly such as relate to character of membership, "jurisdiction" (the prevention of overlapping), the avoidance of duplication of effort and organization, and the adoption of methods for union agitation and education. By a vote of representatives in federation conventions the Federation can, for certain purposes only, impose a slight assessment, a step taken on the rarest occasions. The books of the Federation show how funds raised in this manner, as well as through the regular dues, are expended. They are published in detail in every issue of the American Federationist.

In truth, amidst the clamor raised by financial interest, by partisan prejudice, by sensation-mongers, or through mere shallowness and base truckling to the noise-makers, the country is being compelled to hear the voice of sanity and moral force. That voice is saying that if labor is the basic element in society, the laborer's cause should be sacred to society; if unrestricted competition among wageworkers leads to the frightful deprivation, degeneration and collective slavery of the masses which even America is witnessing, the wage-workers themselves are justified in organized opposition to such competition; if trade unionism as it exists has been the only effective agency de-

veloped to help the masses of wage-workers to get better pay and cut
off the work-hours that destroy health and life, and in general improve the working conditions of labor, encouragement to it is a
national obligation; if it has stood champion for labor's rights, before our legislative bodies, before the public, appealing for whatever
justice can today be had, curbing avarice, performing an unparalleled
work of philanthropy in its mutual benefits—then it deserves to live
and to continue its mission.

Who knows better than the trade unionists themselves the mission
of unionism? How has that mission come to be shaped and developed?
It has come through the free discussion, the public deliberations, the
fairest procedures of a perfectly democratic organization. The voice
and vote of the least man in the last rank has its due force and weight.
Every suggestion from the mind of any and all of the members of a
union has its open channel to reach the full membership. What step
may, or ought, to be taken, in organization, in efficiency, in policy, in
politics, in exclusion or inclusion of members—in all such respects
each union can have its share in proposing and deciding. Hence the
history of the American Federation of Labor is the story of the will
and wish of its majorities. How, then, could it be other than what it
has been? How can it be other than what it is? It rests on the solid
rock of the economic education, the recorded decisions, the deliberate
will of its membership.

Purification? Yes; of whatever evils, of methods or men, that may
appear. That is a natural part of its business, as with every other
institution.

14

Against Imperialism[1]

Gompers and the AFL had an enduring concern with the fate of organized labor in Latin America. The agitation over the Cuban question in the 1890s led to the Spanish-American War, which extended beyond Cuba to the Philippines and Puerto Rico. Gompers joined the Anti-Imperialist League after reluctantly supporting the war in fear that his "Americanism," always precarious and vulnerable to criticism from the Right, be questioned. Earlier in the decade, during the Venezuelan border dispute, it appeared that war might break out between the United States and Great Britain. Gompers attacked the jingo spirit:

Labor is never for war. It is always for peace. It is on the side of liberty, justice and humanity. These three are always for peace. . . . Who would be compelled to bear the burden of a war? The working people. They would pay the taxes, and their blood would flow like water. The interests of the working people of England the United States are common. They are fighting the same enemy. They are battling to emancipate themselves from conditions common to both countries. The working people know no country. They are citizens of the world, and their religion is to do what is right, what is just, what is grand and glorious and valorous and chivalrous. The battle for the cause of labor, from times of remotest antiquity, has been for peace and for good-will among men.

All honor to the brave and valiant soldiers who, by their tact, judgment and heroism, planned and executed the war and brought victory to our arms in a surprisingly brief period! None can pay too glowing tributes to the splendid manifestations and ideal heroism as displayed by Hobson and Wainwright, Miles and Shafter, Wheeler and Lee, and the redoubtable Dewey. And while not detracting one iota from the meed of praise bestowed upon and to which these gallant

[1] From Samuel Gompers' speech at Chicago Peace Jubilee, October 18, 1898. Gompers Papers reprinted in *The American Federationist* (November 1898): 179–83.

men are entitled, yet none the less deserving of the encomiums of praise and honor are the men who carried the guns and "the men behind the guns;" for without their unswerving devotion, their skill, daring and self-sacrifice, victory would have been dashed from our lips and disaster overtaken us all. The honor, the spirit and the valor of American manhood, inspired by American love of liberty, render our people invulnerable in industry, peace and progress, as well as invincible in the art of war. . . .

What the people of our country were unable to accomplish with Spain by peaceable means, we sought to impress upon Congress to achieve by taking up arms against her. Yet, when Congress declared war against the Kingdom of Spain, it, at the same time, declared to the world that the war was begun as "an unselfish endeavor to fulfil a duty to humanity by ending it," and pledged our honor and our faith that there was not on our part "any disposition or intention to exercise sovereignty, jurisdiction or control" over Cuba "except for the pacification thereof." That disclaimer conveyed to the whole world without reserve that we had no selfish purpose in prosecuting this war, and that we were prompted by no desire for annexation or conquest of any territory, near or remote.

What has become of our peans of praise for the brave Cubans? Was our charge against Spain in her refusal to give the people of that island freedom and independence, baseless? If we admit this, we at once confess that our war was without just cause, we confess to a most grievous wrong committed. Where is the spirit of holding out the helping hand in aid of all people struggling for liberty and independence? Where has flown this great outburst of our sympathy for the self-sacrificing and liberty-loving Cubans? Is it not strange that now, for the first time, we hear that the Cubans are unfit for self-government; that whether they protest against it or not, they must be dominated by us, annexed to us or become a dependency of ours?

Alas! there are some Americans—our money makers—whose only god is the almighty dollar, whose only human or divine trinity is dividend, interest and profit, come to the conclusion that if poor, suffering Cuba can be handed over to their tender mercies, their deity and their deviltry can hold full sway. These gentry, when there is a question between liberty and profit, present or prospective liberty is thrown to the dogs as a wornout and threadbare thing of the past.

If we have intervened in behalf of Cuba, and driven a foreign tyrant from her shores, we have at least authority for our action by the appeals of the struggling Cubans. But what of the Porto Ricans? They have not asked our intervention; they have not pleaded for annexation. Their country was invaded as a military necessity. They number eight hundred thousand people, and have not been divided by fierce conflict. If we give freedom and independence to Cuba, to which she is entitled, is there any justification for our enforced conquest and annexation of Porto Rico?

Hawaii we have annexed, irrespective of the wishes of her people, who were not asked whether the constitution under which they have recently lived meets with their approval. Nor was annexation, in its direct or indirect form, ever given to them for decision. The flag of our country waves in Hawaii over a people, subjugated by our superior force, in flagrant violation of the consent of the governed.

In the case of the Philippines we have the question repeated, only in a much more aggravated form. The circumstances of war gave the opportunity for the destruction of the Spanish fleet at Manila. We found the Filipinos, however, in arms for freedom from Spain and the independence of their country. Our aid was neither sought nor requested. We proclaimed the high motives with which we entered into the struggle with Spain; and yet, the first moment we have the opportunity of laying our hands upon territory which we invade as a chance of war, we are at once asked to violate every declaration which we have made, or promise which we have given, and insist that these islands, with their subjugated people, shall come under our domination. Are we in a moment, filled with the delirium of triumph, to turn our backs upon our entire past and all that has made us great and respected? I trust not. . . .

There is even now a strife going on among the nations of the earth for the partition and possession of Eastern countries. Let us take the Philippines, and we shall be in the midst of the conflicts. We shall have to follow the monarchical policy of large standing armies, with immense navies (not always voluntary). We shall not only have to bear the heavy burdens of debt and taxation exceeding those of other nations, but we will come to that point against which the genius of our institutions revolts—compulsory military duty.

It will not be amiss to call attention to some of the conditions prevailing in the islands, which the thoughtless enthusiast and the grab-all monopolist commercial spirit of our day, urge us to annex. We should know the dangers which are involved in the silly or wicked policy of imperialism and expansion.

With less than one hundred thousand inhabitants in Hawaii, fifty thousand are contract laborers, practically slaves. Of this number there are fully eighty per cent. Chinese and Japanese, twenty per cent. South Sea Islanders and Portuguese from the Azore Islands. The terms of contract of these slave laborers run for seven years. The laborers have no right either to change their employers or leave their employment; the contract to labor is specifically enforced by law. Any time a laborer may serve in imprisonment by reason of his failure to perform the work required is added to the life of the contract to labor; that is, after his term of imprisonment has expired, he must work that same length of time, in order to fill out the time of the contract. . . .

And such is the make-up of the eight millions of the inhabitants of the Philippines—Malays, Negritos and Chinamen, the semi-barbaric peoples of the more than three hundred islands comprising the group in the Archipelago who are to come within the fold of our Union. What a wonderful achievement; what a marvelous gain to the civilization of America.

Recently, giving vent to the first evidence of civilizing influences (the Filipinos near Manila, suffering severely from the increased cost of living as a result of the war), some workers requested a paltry increase in wages. As a substitute some of these poor fellows were forced back to work at the point of the bayonet; others, who were more stubborn, were run through, and some cast into dungeons.

If we attempt to force upon the natives of the Philippines our rule, and compel them to conform to our more or less rigid form of government, how many lives shall we take? Of course, they will seem cheap, because they are poor laborers. They will be members of the majority in the Philippines, but they will be ruled and killed at the convenience of the very small minority there, backed up by our armed land and sea forces. The dominant class in the islands will ease its conscience because the victims will be poor, ignorant and weak. When innocent men can be shot down on the public highway as they were in Lattimer, Penn., and Virden, Ill., men of our own flesh ad blood, men who help to make this homogeneous nation great, because they dare ask for more humane conditions at the hands of the moneyed class of our country, how much more difficult will it be to arouse any sympathy, and secure relief for the poor semi-savages in the Philippines, much less indignation at any crime against their inherent and natural rights to life, liberty and the pursuit of happiness?

If the Philippines are annexed, what is to prevent the Chinese, the Negritos and the Malays coming to our country? How can we prevent the Chinese coolies from going to the Philippines and from there swarming into the United States engulfing our people and our civilization. If these new islands are to become ours, it will be either under the form of Territories or States. Can we hope to close the flood-gates of immigration from the hordes of Chinese and the semi-savage races coming from what will then be part of our own country? Certainly, if we are to retain the principles of law enunciated from the foundation of our Government, no legislation of such a character can be expected.

In a country such as ours the conditions and opportunities of the wage earners are profoundly affected by the view of the worth or dignity of men who earn their bread by the work of their hands. The progress and improvement in the condition of the wage earners in the former slave States have been seriously obstructed for decades in which manual labor and slave labor were identical. The South now, with difficulty, respects labor, because labor is the condition of those who were formerly slaves, and this fact operates potentially against any effort to secure social justice by legislative action or organized movement of the workers. If these facts have operated so effectually to prevent necessary changes in the condition of our own people, how difficult will it be to quicken our conscience so as to secure social and legislative relief for the semi-savage slave or contract laborers of the conquered islands?

15

War Letter to Workers and Soldiers of Russia[1]

The collapse of the Czarist regime in March 1917 threatened to end the war on the eastern front, permitting German armies to concentrate against the western Allies, including the United States, which entered the war in April. Gompers, a strong supporter of Wilson, urged the newly formed soviets to sustain the prowar Kerensky government against the defeatist Bolsheviks who hoped to turn the war into revolution. The Russians continued fighting and lost repeatedly. Discontent grew and in October the Bolsheviks overthrew Kerensky and stopped fighting, making a separate peace with the Germans.

WASHINGTON, *May 6, 1917*

WORKMEN'S AND SOLDIERS' COUNCIL OF DEPUTIES, Petrograd, Russia.

The gravest crisis in the world's history is now hanging in the balance, and the course which Russia will pursue may have a determining influence whether democracy or autocracy shall prevail. That democracy and freedom will finally prevail there can be no doubt in the minds of men who know, but the cost, the time lost and the sacrifices which would ensue from lack of united action may be appalling. It is to avoid this that I address you.

In view of the grave crisis through which the Russian people are passing we assure you that you can rely absolutely upon the wholehearted support and co-operation of the American people in the great war against our common enemy, Kaiserism. In the fulfillment of that cause the present American government has the support of 99 percent of the American people, including the working class of both the cities and the agricultural sections.

In free America, as in free Russia, the agitators for a peace favorable to Prussian militarism have been allowed to express their opinions so that the conscious and unconscious tools of the Kaiser appear

[1] From Samuel Gompers, *Labor and the War* (Washington, D. C., 1918).

more influential than they really are. You should realize the truth of the situation. There are but few in America willing to allow Kaiserism and its allies to continue their rule over those non-German peoples who wish to be free from their domination. Should we not protest against the pro-Kaiser Socialist interpretation of the demand for no annexation, namely, that all oppressed non-German peoples shall be compelled to remain under the domination of Prussia and her lackeys —Austria and Turkey? Should we not rather accept the better interpretation that there must be no forcible annexations, but that every people must be free to choose any allegiance it desires, as demanded by the Council of Worker's and Soldiers' Deputies?

Like yourselves, we are opposed to all punitive and improper indemnities. We denounce the onerous punitive indemnities already imposed by the Kaiser upon the people of Serbia, Belgium and Poland.

America's workers share the view of the Council of Workmen's and Soldiers' Deputies that the only way in which the German people can bring the war to an early end is by imitating the glorious example of the Russian people, compelling the abdication of the Hohenzollerns and the Hapsburgs, and driving the tyrannous nobility, bureaucracy and the military castes from power.

Let the German Socialists attend to this, and cease their false pretenses and underground plotting to bring about an abortive peace in the interest of Kaiserism and the ruling class. Let them cease calling pretended "international" conferences at the instigation or connivance of the Kaiser. Let them cease their intrigues to cajole the Russian and American working people to interpret your demand, "No annexations, no indemnities," in a way to leave undiminished the prestige and the power of the German military caste.

Now that Russian autocracy is overthrown, neither the American government nor the American people apprehend that the wisdom and experience of Russia in the coming constitutional assembly will adopt any form of government other than the one best suited to your needs. We feel confident that no message, no individual emissary and no commission has been sent, or will be sent, with authority to offer any advice whatever to Russia as to the conduct of her internal affairs. Any commission that may be sent will help Russia in any way that she desires to combat Kaiserism wherever it exists or may manifest itself.

Word has reached us that false reports of an American purpose and of American opinions contrary to the above statement have gained some circulation in Russia. We denounce these reports as the criminal work of desperate pro-Kaiser propagandists, circulated with the intent to deceive and to arouse hostile feelings between the two great democracies of the world. The Russian people should know that these activities are only additional manifestations of the "dark forces" with which Russia has been only too familiar in the unhappy past.

The American government, the American people, the American labor movement are whole-heartedly with the Russian workers, the Russian masses in the great effort to maintain the freedom you have already achieved and to solve the grave problems yet before you. We earnestly appeal to you to make common cause with us to abolish and maintain for generations yet unborn the priceless treasures of justice, freedom, democracy and humanity.

16
Against Bolshevism[1]

Gompers' opposition to the second Russian Revolution, led by Lenin and Trotsky, continued after the close of the First World War. By 1921, when it appeared that the Bolsheviks had consolidated power, Gompers opposed both recognition of and resumption of trade with the Soviet Union. Gompers claimed that in Soviet Russia "the workers are conscripted into the army and into industry. There is no such thing as collective bargaining. In fact, no bargain is made. It is compulsion. . . . Soviet authorities have by decree forbidden organizations of labor to exercise those functions without which labor is powerless. To strike in Russia today is to be guilty of sedition and [to face] death." [2]

When he published Out of Their Own Mouths: A Revelation and an Indictment of Sovietism, *the* Locomotive Engineers Journal—*a normally conservative union magazine—criticized him for his narrow-minded petulence and his failure to sympathize with a "workers government." "While American labor is being crucified," the* Journal *charged, "Mr. Gompers takes time to stick pins into the hide of the Russian bear."* [3] *The following essay is drawn from Gompers' introduction to* Out of Their Own Mouths.

I have been under the necessity of observing the Bolshevist movement from close quarters for many years. I have had to contend with it almost daily long before it seized the power in Russia in the name of Communism and Soviet. Trotsky is only one of the Bolshevist leaders who long sojourned in this country to plague the American labor movement. And the few thousands who have returned to Soviet Russia represent but a small part of the forces of revolutionary mania in

[1] From Samuel Gompers and William English Walling, *Out of Their Own Mouths: A Revelation and an Indictment of Sovietism* (New York: E. P. Dutton, 1921), pp. v–ix.

[2] Philip Taft, *The A. F. of L. in the Time of Gompers* (New York: Harper & Row, Inc., 1957), p. 449.

[3] As quoted in Philip S. Foner, *The Bolshevik Revolution: Its Impact on American Radicals, Liberals, and Labor* (New York: International Publishers Co., Inc., 1967), p. 49.

America. These forces are not strong enough seriously to threaten American labor—provided they are isolated and understood. But they must be understood and isolated.

While the labor movement of the world is gradually but steadily shaking itself free of the illusion that the Soviets are a workingmen's government—the first workingmen's government—conservative powers are beginning to give them commercial and political support and a part of the press is engaged in finding virtuous reasons for this policy. The pace was set by the British-Soviet trade agreement and by Lloyd George's speech in Parliament in which he contended, with an intentional paradox but still quite seriously, that the Bolshevists had suddenly become moderates. The work of labor in repudiating Bolshevism has thus become more difficult. Certain conservatives and reactionaries pretend—for motives of their own—that they no longer have much objection to the Soviets. They are willing to trade with cannibals, to use an expression of Lloyd George. But labor cannot affiliate or associate with cannibals—or with tyrants who rule over labor by the Red Terror and the firing squad.

Whether an anti-labor despotism rules over one of the greatest peoples of the earth may be a matter of indifference to the masters of the British Empire as long as that despotism is willing to meet the Empire half way—and to sign away the title to the territories and natural wealth of the nation. It cannot be a matter of indifference to labor.

Labor's interest in putting forth the truth about the Soviets is in part altruistic. Labor's regard for the welfare of the Russian workers is deep and genuine. But it also knows that if an anti-labor despotism may be made to work in one country—however inefficiently—it will encourage the enemies of labor to try the same methods elsewhere. Moreover, if the Soviets are given a certain parmanence and success as "moderates" by the aid of certain governments and financiers they will certainly continue to represent this success to the labor of the world as having come to them from their own efforts as "ultra-revolutionists."

The outward success of the Soviets—with capitalist backing—would cost the capitalists themselves dearly in the end. But labor would pay, and pay heavily from the beginning.

The Soviets may or may not reach a common understanding of real practical importance with cynical imperialists and capitalistic adventurers. There is no possible common ground between Bolshevism and organized labor. Nor will the proposed economic alliance between Bolshevism and Reaction be able to force labor to compromise with the Soviets. In the long run this alliance will help to make still more clear to the wage-earners the true character of Bolshevism. But its first result is to re-inforce the already formidable Bolshevist propaganda.

I must take this opportunity to point out that the hostility of the Bolshevists to the American Federation of Labor is of the same degree of intensity and of the same general character as the hostility of a large group of reactionary employers—a group to be found in all countries, but at the present moment far more aggressive and powerful in the United States than in any other nation of the globe. So closely identical are the anti-labor-union policies of the Bolshevists and Reactionaries that a number of instances have already arisen of deliberate cooperation to destroy organized labor. But even when there is no definite alliance the similarity of the purposes and methods of the two groups bring it about that they spread an identical propaganda. The Reactionary, therefore, does not disguise the delight with which he reads of the Bolshevist attacks on organized labor, nor do the Bolshevists disguise their joy at the victories of Reaction. Nor is this the only way by which Reaction aids Bolshevism; in its refusal to grant reasonable economic concessions and to cede to reasonable demands for political and legislative reforms, the Reactionaries inevitably drive the thoughtless and impatient into the arms of Bolshevism.

17

On Fascism

Although he condemned both fascism and bolshevism on similar grounds ("The historic tendency of autocracy," he wrote, "is always to perpetuate and enlarge its existing powers"), Gompers feared Lenin's Reds more than Mussolini's Black Shirts. In 1923, while reviewing a book on Italian fascism, Gompers remarked that the "political franchise" was gradually being replaced by an "industrial franchise." Dictatorships and autocracies were hardly attractive, Gompers wrote, but "American trade unionists will at least find it possible to have some sympathy with the policies of a man [Mussolini] whose dominating purpose is to get something done; to do rather than to theorize; to build a working, producing civilization instead of a disorganized, theorizing aggregation of conflict groups."

The following statements are drawn from Gompers' last writings in The American Federationist.

AN ANALYSIS OF FASCISM [1]

Mussolini as the dominant figure of the Fascist movement has talked and acted like a thorough-going reactionary and it is only a close analysis of what lies behind his movements and of what is written into the Fascist program and philosophy that reveals the constructive side of the movement that now governs Italy. . . .

It must of course be understood that at the time the Fascisti came into power in Italy and for sometime prior thereto there had been a rising and dangerous Bolshevik movement, fostered under the direct guidance of the Moscow authorities. The best information available is that had the Fascisti not seized the government just when they did the Bolsheviks would have done so not many days later. . . .

The author tells us that the Fascisti look forward to a society "whose permanent and characteristic feature will be the collaboration among the various classes and functions for the common good, and

[1] From *The American Federationist* 30 (November 1923): 927-33.

their aim is to start this collaboration at once and to make of it a practical method of nationbuilding."

It will be surprising to many Americans, and agreeably so to some, to learn that at least in the author's view the two most important reforms that Fascism is urging at present are: Vocational parliaments and a system of suitable and efficient government.

One can not escape the conviction after reading the book that if the political franchise is for the moment a somewhat innocuous institution there is in the process of development an industrial franchise which with the promised revival of the political franchise will give the Italian people a voice in the conduct of their daily affairs such as they have never enjoyed before.

Surely political Italy was in an amazing state of disorganization prior to the Fascisti revolution. Perhaps Americans find it difficult to comprehend a political situation such as that which existed in Italy where the parliamentary system had become little more than a joke so far as the masses of the people were concerned and merely the means to a more or less precarious livelihood so far as the politicians were concerned.

The Fascisti movement is intensely national and perhaps its first principle is that national unity is essential. It has been said freely by critics of the Fascisti, and not without reason, that the movement has had a strong and bitter anti-labor bias. This the author denies. He says the Fascisti understand fully that no government can be permanent that is in opposition to the proletariat, "just as it would be out of the question to sacrifice completely the bourgeoisie or the propertied classes."

"Fascism," says Por, "is revolutionary, not because it seized power by illegal means, but because by means of its dictatorship it is constructing a functional democracy." . . .

However repugnant may be the idea of dictatorship and the man on horseback, American trade unionists will at least find it possible to have some sympathy with the policies of a man whose dominating purpose is to get something done; to do rather than to theorize; to build a working, producing civilization instead of a disorganized, theorizing aggregation of conflicting groups.

In Italy industrial councils composed of all elements represented in industry are demanded in the platform and program of the Fascist organization. One of the complaints of the Fascisti against the labor organizations as they were prior to the advent of the Mussolini government was the overwhelmingly political character of those organizations. It must be conceded that there was much justice in the Fascisti contention. The Italian unions had concerned themselves much more with political questions and political methods than with industrial questions and industrial methods, to the undoubted detriment of the Italian wage earners.

The American Federation of Labor has not accepted the Fascisti regime as a great exponent of democracy. It came into power by methods that in themselves constituted a renunciation of democracy and it has proclaimed upon more than one occasion its defiance of democratic methods. Allowance must be made, however, for conditions which surrounded the growth of the Fascist organization and its attainment of power. The effectiveness of parliamentary action had been largely destroyed. This was apparently due partly to Communist intrigue. The government itself had been reduced almost to impotence and was used much more as a means to personal power and aggrandizement than as a means to national welfare and development.

[EDITORIAL] 2

The government of Italy at present is in power as a result of a mandate from the people, expressed through an election, and what has passed can not discount what is to come if it is of constructive, democratic character.

The supremacy of industrial life, long recognized by American labor, is becoming more and more clear to European wage earners, partly, no doubt, as a result of their repeated failure to usher in a much heralded new era through political action. If the European methods of developing self-government in industry differ from those methods which American trade unionists believe should be adopted in our own country, we must concede the right of the wage earners of each country to adopt those methods which in their own circumstances and conditions seem best adapted to achieve the desired results. We must concede to them the right even to make the most serious mistakes.

Whether right or wrong the developments now taking place and to which attention has here been called are of the most important character and they will be followed everywhere with the deepest interest.

² From *The American Federationist* 31 (July 1924): 565–69.

GOMPERS VIEWED BY HIS CONTEMPORARIES

> "Had Mr. Gompers been able to add six inches to his height, he would have been one of our great tragedians."
>
> —"Recollections of John Frey," *Washington Herald*, September 5, 1938.

On the morning of March 31, 1901, the Washington train pulled into the Danville, Virginia, station. A fairly large crowd of the town's union and civic establishment assembled on the platform. A large band, all members of the Musicians' Union, waited. Down the steps of the lead car stepped a short, balding, stocky man, "incredibly ugly, his arms seeming to reach below his knees, ape fashion." [1] The band struck up a presidential "Hail to the Chief" and the distinguished crowd cheered. Samuel Gompers had arrived to lecture on behalf of organized labor. His speech, reported at great length by the local papers, was on the eleven commandments, the new commandment being: "Thou shalt not take thy neighbor's job." [2] Whether lecturing on labor's cause, testifying before congressional groups, or meeting the press during a crisis, Gompers "appeared" before a national audience for nearly fifty years.

Much of Gompers' success was due to his intuitive sense of importance, an actor's timing, and a grave, barrel-voiced, platform eloquence. Arriving in San Francisco in 1891 where the current labor issue involved the use of nonunion Chinese cigarmakers, he greeted a reporter with the gift of a handmade cigar, rolled that morning by the president of the AFL himself. And the journalist told his readers how, "we enjoyed the cigar. It was white labor-made, by a white man, one of nature's own noblemen. Such is Samuel Gompers." [3] When he left San Francisco, a labor delegation presented him with a farewell poem:

---

[1] Papers of John Frey, Library of Congress.
[2] Danville (Virginia) *Register*, March 31, 1901.
[3] San Francisco *Star*, March 14, 1891.

*"The American Federation of Labor is the cause
of additions to our Statutes of Reformed Labor Laws
And down the distant ages our
Gompers' name shall
go
As bright as the happy smiles
He caused around our
Hearth to
glow."* [4]

*Gompers was not always received so well. Over the years his
enemies accumulated, and his long record of power bruised old
and nagging wounds. "Big Bill" Haywood of the Western Federation of Miners (and later the IWW) considered Gompers something of a bad joke, a "squat specimen of humanity":*

*It was amusing to see the big, broad-shouldered men of the
West, [Haywood wrote in his autobiography] taking the measure of this undersized individual. . . . Sam was very short and
chunky with a big head that was bald in patches, resembling a
child suffering with ringworm. He had small snapping eyes, a
hard cruel mouth, wide with thin drooping lips, heavy jaws
and jowels, a personality vain, conceited, petulant and vindic-
tive.*

*Looking at him, I could realize the passion of cruelty with
which this person would wield power if he had it. It was easy
to understand how Gompers could plead for men who were
facing the noose of the executioners—with his tongue in his
cheek and his heart reeking with hypocrisy. One could realize
that he might even refer jokingly to the defeat of a great labor
struggle, if it were being conducted by an organization that
was not strictly in accordance with his views. To look at him
was to know that he could protest against giving relief to
women and children.*[5]

*Clever cartoons were used to depict the absurdity of Gompers
by sketching his short, disproportioned figure as if it were the
embodiment of his ideas. A leading socialist paper*[6] *caricatured
Gompers as a dog, with a dollar sign for a tail, blocking the
bridge leading to socialism.* American Industry, *the NAM official*

[4] Ibid.
[5] *Bill Haywood's Book: The Autobiography of William D. Haywood* (New York:
International Publishers Co., Inc., 1929), pp. 72–73.
[6] *Chicago Socialist,* August 30, 1902.

publication, frequently showed Gompers as the stereotyped Jewish menace hovering over private property.

The following selections indicate the variety and intensity of responses Gompers provoked in nearly fifty years of glaring public exposure.

18

Bernard Mandel: Gompers at Work[7]

In 1896, the A. F. of L. decided to give up its isolated headquarters in Indianapolis and move to the District of Columbia, where the officers could give more direct attention to their legislative program. Gompers packed up again and went to the nation's capital, then a small provincial city with a distinct Southern flavor. He rented a home on H Street, N. E.—a two-story brick home in a row-building, its narrow front facing directly on the sidewalk—and brought his family down from New York. But for a number of years he regarded his residence in Washington as temporary, maintaining his legal address in New York and going back each year to vote. Since Washingtonians were disfranchised, Gompers felt that to make the capital his legal residence would be an act of expatriation. Besides, he was fond of the metropolis: "too good a place to 'swear off.' "

In the next few years, a series of misfortunes struck Gompers' family. In 1898, while he was in Omaha for a Labor Day address, his mother died. She had become quite helpless in her old age, and lived in Samuel's apartment in New York. Since it was not possible for him to return to New York in time for the funeral, his family did not notify him of her death until his return. Gompers' father, Solomon, then came to Washington to stay with him, along with three of Samuel's still unmarried children. A few months later, Gompers was again in the far West, attending a labor rally in Des Moines. He was introduced by the chairman of the board of public works in place of the mayor, who was unable to be present because of the death of his

[7] From Bernard Mandel, *Samuel Gompers: A Biography* (Yellow Springs, Ohio: The Antioch Press, 1963), pp. 165–70. Reprinted by permission of Kent State University Press.

daughter the day before. Gompers prefaced his speech with a few words of condolence to the mayor and his family. He then proceeded with his address, in the course of which a messenger came on the platform and placed a telegram on the table next to him.

Gompers concluded his point, picked up the telegram, tossed it aside, then picked it up again and opened it. Before reading it, he started to speak again: "Wages, after all, find their own level—." There was silence in the theatre as he read the message, tried to resume his speech, but was unable to pick up the thread of his argument. He asked the audience to excuse him for a few moments. The chairman addressed the audience for a few minutes, and then determined to dismiss the meeting. Gompers returned to the stage and explained:

"I exceedingly regret that I should thus disappoint this audience. Never before in my work have I disappointed my audience in failing to complete my address. The telegram which was dropped upon the table tells me to come at once, as my eldest daughter is very low. It means more than that to me, for I know that my family, desiring to encourage my work as much as possible, would not wire me unless the very worst had occurred. It means that I have no hope. I trust you will excuse me, and that some time I may again visit your city and speak to the people."

When Gompers got home, Rose was dead. He brought her two children home to live with him and Sophia. A year later his son Abe contracted tuberculosis and had to go West to try to recover his health. He was able to work for a while, but soon became too weak to continue. It was necessary to give him greater care and more expensive treatment, and Gompers was without funds. Max Morris, the president of the retail clerks' union, who was living in Denver, arranged to take care of the boy and to foot the bills until Gompers was able to repay him. Abe died after two years' illness. Gompers owed Morris about $2,000 and in order to pay the debt, he contracted for a series of ten lectures on the Chautauqua circuit.

In 1902, Gompers' son Al married and it was planned to have him and his wife live at his home, so more room was needed. Gompers bought a house on First Street, N. W., for $5,700: a large, six-room, stone-front building. The living room was small, with a few old-fashioned chairs covered with linen, a piano for Sadie, a bust of Gompers, four or five paintings on the walls, and some bric-a-brac distributed over the room. There was an artificial fireplace on one wall, and the room was heated with a parlor stove. The third floor was fitted up as a workroom and library, where Gompers often worked until three in the morning; his granddaughter Florence studied typing and stenography so she could help.

The Gompers household was a constellation which revolved entirely around the "old man," as Sam was already known by his friends. "Mamma" lived only to make him happy, and she catered to his every whim. Short, plump, and motherly, her world was encompassed in her home, her family, and her husband. While Gompers had educated himself, Sophia remained the simple housewife, who knew, however, what unionism meant to a worker and understood that her husband had a big job in the labor movement. She had endured years of poverty and loneliness, but never complained: helping Sam, she was content.

Gompers' youngest daughter, Sadie, was the apple of his eye. When there were guests, she was the hostess, as she had an urbanity and brightness that were lacking in Mamma. Her father had great hopes of an operatic career for her. She had been encouraged by her music teacher in school, and Gompers provided singing lessons for her for seven years. In 1906, she went on a vaudeville tour for the Keith circuit. Mamma always accompanied her, either because she did not want to travel alone, as Gompers wrote, or because he insisted on it, as his granddaughter says. Sadie decided to give up her career so that her mother could stay at home and be with Sam. It is doubtful if the sacrifice was a great one, for her talents were over-rated, and a large part of her audiences was made up of people who were curious to see Gompers' daughter on the stage and workers who were urged to go to the theatre to give their chief's daughter a break.

When Gompers was in the city, there was often company at his home. Many times he would bring associates home for dinner, so that they could discuss labor matters, and often they would come even for breakfast to get an early start on the day's work. James O'Connell, the president of the International Association of Machinists and a vice-president of the Federation, was a neighbor and frequent visitor. Tom Tracy, a cigarmaker and later an organizer and member of the legislative committee in Washington, was another close friend who often came to his home. Others for whom Gompers had a particular attachment were George Perkins, president of the cigarmakers' union, and John O'Sullivan, whom the Gomperses called their "son." But they were only occasional visitors, as they did not live in Washington. Besides his family and friends in the labor movement, there were many others whom Gompers entertained at home. There were convivial gatherings with his Elks brothers, visits by politicians, clergymen, and industrialists, and many parties for actors who were playing in Washington. Gompers became acquainted with many actors, singers, and chorus girls, as he often went to the same restaurants and bars after meetings, when they were coming from the theater. He also met some through his cousin, Sam Collins, who was a well-known comedian.

When Gompers was at home, Sunday was always open house. He

expected every member of the family who was in the city to visit him, and friends were always there too. They would talk, play penny ante, or listen to music. Gompers was very fond of music, and had one of the first Victor machines and a fine collection of records. At these gatherings, Gompers always insisted on occupying the center of the stage. If some one else seemed to be attracting the attention of the group, he would step in and steal the show. These were his parties, it was his home, and he wanted to be the "big man."

When he could not go home to dinner because of evening work at his office or elsewhere, Gompers generally dined at Perreard's, a French theatrical boarding house and restaurant. The proprietor, known as "The Count," and his wife presided over the festivities, introducing the guests to each other as "Citizen So-and-so," and often entertaining by singing. The restaurant was frequented by French citizens, ambassadors, and reporters, actors and actresses, and intellectuals and *bon vivants* from all countries. On Bastille Day each year, the regular patrons, known as the "reptiles," were invited to a special ceremony, with Gompers as guest of honor. In the small back court, covered with latticework and vines, the birthday of the French Republic was celebrated with more than the usual quantities of "red ink."

For all his family spirit and his devotion to his brothers and children, Gompers consistently refused to use his influence to help them. When he first came to Washington, both of his unmarried sons were unemployed. Henry was a stone mason and Al a painter whose hands were weakened by disease. Yet Gompers would not give them work in the Federation mailing room. Years later, Al besought him for an appointment from Herman Robinson, Gompers' former organizer in New York who was then New York commissioner of licenses. Gompers would not make the request. He felt that if he were to have any influence with men in public office, he had to remain absolutely independent of any obligations to them. He also had to avoid anything that might be interpreted as misuse of his office. One day he came to his office and found that his granddaughter Florence had secured a job there as a stenographer. He immediately ordered her discharge.

By the turn of the century, Gompers' physical appearance had changed markedly since his advent to the presidency of the American Federation of Labor a decade and a half earlier. His intemperate eating and drinking showed itself in stoutness to such an extent that vaudeville comedians drew laughs by patting their bellies and referring to them as their "Sam Gompers." Following the national trend in styles, he had shaved his walrus mustache and goateé, revealing the very wide mouth with its turned-down corners and prominent lower lip. As a result of the attack of eczema which he suffered in 1896, his large face was pock-marked and his graying hair had begun to fall out in patches. Mark Sullivan observed that his hair looked "like a piece of worn-out buffalo robe which has lain in the garret and been chewed by the moths since 1890, and then been thrown out in the rain and laid in the gutter for a year or two, and been dragged back by a puppy dog to cut his teeth on." In order to hide this condition, Gompers (like John D. Rockefeller) took to wearing a black skullcap, or *yamelka*. He almost invariably wore it in his office, and when he went out he put it in his pocket for later use. Occasionally he wore it even at public appearances when addressing meetings or testifying before legislative committees. His weakening eyes caused him to begin wearing glasses about this time, which added to his middle-aged appearance.

Gompers' appearance seemed to depend largely on the observer's attitude toward him. Walter Gordon Merritt, a writer for an anti-union employers' association, saw him for the first time about 1902 and was impressed with the qualities which he thought would "inspire a small-town boy with fear and admiration. Wholly un-American in appearance; short; with large eyes, dark complexion, heavy-lined face, and hair slightly curly but looking moth-eaten—he was impressive. As I sat in the audience . . . I wrote the name 'Marat' on a slip of paper and handed it to my companion. He nodded." . . .

As the influence of the A. F. of L. grew, Gompers became a prominent figure in the public eye, the object of frequent comment and cartoons in the press, a speaker at important meetings, a witness before congressional committees, a friend of politicians, industrialists, and social leaders. He became more self-conscious and self-impressed. He began to dress more carefully than he had in his youth, even nattily, with a diamond pin in his cravat. His bearing was one of great dignity—some thought he was cocky and a show-off. Among his friends he was Sam Gompers the cigarmaker, one of the boys, a hail-fellow-well-met, bubbling over with fun and affability, a good story teller, and a congenial companion. But when he appeared as Samuel Gompers, president of the American Federation of Labor, he was a different man—"calm, dignified, and unapproachable, jealously resenting anything and everything that would detract from the dignity of the position he holds."

On one occasion he called at the White House to express to Theodore Roosevelt his displeasure at a public statement made by the latter. He spoke so vigorously that Roosevelt, showing irritation, hit the desk with his fist and said, "Mr. Gompers, I want you to understand, sir, that I am the President of the United States." Gompers faced him with blazing eyes, and hitting the desk with equal emphasis, shot back, "Mr. President, I want you to understand that I am the president of the American Federation of Labor."

While he was becoming middle-aged, dignified, and respectable, he did not slow down. His energy was tireless, and his constitution apparently impervious to abuse. He took a Rabelaisian joy in the pleasures of life, and his work was one of those pleasures. He became more intemperate in his drinking, and sometimes became drunk even in public. After dinner or an evening meeting, he often went out to "take a walk" which invariably brought him to a saloon. At conventions, he would get roaring drunk nearly every night after the session was adjourned, but the next morning he appeared on the platform fit, clear, and ready for business. John Frey once reproved him for drinking too much, and Gompers said, "Well, John, we're all different in our make-up. When I have to think a great deal I become tense, and the only way I can relax is to take a few drinks." He was equally regardless of the rules of common sense in matters of diet, sleep, pleasure and work. Even his relaxation, which he often took in one of the cheap burlesque houses on Pennsylvania Avenue, was of the same pattern.

His schedule of work was onerous. He seldom traveled less than 10,000 miles a year, sometimes 25,000, making as many as 150 addresses in the course of a year and appearing at twenty-five to fifty hearings before congressional, state, and municipal committees. He held hundreds of conferences yearly with labor men, representatives of other organizations, employers, and congressmen. His activities during one month were typical. The Federation convention in New Orleans adjourned at three in the morning on November 23, 1902. The same day he held a conference with representatives of various labor organizations and a meeting with the Executive Council. Two days later he was in Birmingham to address a mass meeting. He returned to Washington on the 28th, and four days later went to Hartford, Connecticut, to attempt to adjust a dispute between the Horse Nail Makers Union and the Capewell Horse Nail Company. The following day he was in Boston, where on successive evenings he lectured at Faneuil Hall and debated with Louis D. Brandeis on the incorporation of unions. Stopping at New York to address the National Civic Federation, he returned to the capital to make two appearances before a Senate committee considering the eight-hour bill. He went back to New York the next day to lecture on strikes to the League for Political Education, returned to Washington, and stayed only a few hours, when he was called to Scranton to testify before the Anthracite Coal Strike Commission. He returned to his office on December 18. During that month he sent out some 5,000 letters, of which he probably dictated 500 personally. . . .

19
The Wife of a Scab (1900)[1]

Opposition to unionization came from most employers and some workers. The following testimony before the Industrial Commission of 1900 is by the formidable wife of a non-union Chicago painter. Her husband, she said, "has incurred the enmity of the house painters' union, simply by protecting the interests of his employers."

Q. Has he ever sought entrance into the union?—A. He has sought entrance into the union. There was a fine entered against him of $100. He had been a member of the union twice.

Q. What was the offense?—A. The offense was going one Sunday and putting in a skylight over some $7,000 worth of fine electrical machinery while the work was on a strike. There was a star-chamber meeting called and a fine was entered against him of $100. He refused to pay it, consequently a vote of expulsion was taken. The contractors were Angus & Gindele, general contractors.

Q. Had he violated the rule?—A. That was the law. He worked, while there was a strike, in protecting the interests of his employer while putting in that skylight to prevent the destruction of thousands of dollars worth of fine electrical machinery at the power house of the West Side Union Traction Building. That was his offense.

Q. Has his employer not taken care of him since then?—A. Employers don't do those things—not Chicago employers. They laid for him, as they say, some six or seven men, in the halls of that power house, and beat him into insensibility. The policeman (turning her back to the commissioners) never saw it; very conveniently turned his back— policeman on the corner; I have forgotten now his name. Two men coming through the hall saved his life. They beat and kicked him into insensibility.

Q. (*By Mr. Clarke.*) Did he know who did it?—A. Entertainment committee; that is all.

[1] From *Report of the [U. S.] Industrial Commission on the Chicago Labor Disputes of 1900* (Washington, D. C., 1901), vol. 8, pp. 79–82.

Q. Did he ever institute any prosecution?—A. The man was frightened out of his life. He would not allow me to see a lawyer to enter suit. I must have my living taken away from me. I am an American woman. I am not disposed to be thrown on charity. I have had to have coal brought to my house because I had none. I considered I was taking work from some woman that had no protector, when I have a husband who is able and willing to support me, and who has always had, when he has been at work, the very highest rate of wages, regardless of unions or any other corporation, because his employers considered him worthy of it.

Q. Do you wish us to understand that he was intimidated?—A. Certainly. The man is afraid of his life. Now, if he knew I was here this afternoon he would want to leave town to-night, if he had to walk.

Q. (By Mr. Kennedy.) He will read it in the papers in the morning.—A. Let him read it; I will stand for it. I went to the painter's union at one time and I told them I wanted them to allow my husband to work and support me; that he was able and willing to work, and I did not propose to be turned on charity by such people; that I was an American woman and as an American woman wanted my support in its proper channel.

Q. (By Mr. Clarke.) What answer did you get?—A. They let him alone for a few months.

Q. Let him work?—A. Let him work.

Q. (By Mr. Kennedy.) Did they call him a scab?—A. They called him a scab.

Q. Have you any children?—A. No.

Q. Does the fact that they call him a scab affect you socially?—A. Doesn't affect me socially, because I consider it is an honor to be independent. I am the one that has had to suffer, instead of having the comforts that I should have as an American woman. As my husband is a citizen and a voter and has had honorary service through the civil war and 5 years in the regular army—George Washington's Own—if that does not entitle him to protection under the Constitution of these United States in supporting me, is there any place in the world where there is protection?

Q. (By Mr. Clarke.) Do you feel that adequate police protection is afforded in case of these labor difficulties?—A. Adequate police protection is an unknown quantity, in a measure. Different minds have different opinions as to what adequate police protection is. During the Debs strike I saw policemen wearing white ribbons.

Q. What did that mean?—A. That was the American Railway Union emblem; it was also the Christian Temperance emblem. They were wearing the white ribbon in sympathy for the Debs organization. If the police and union labor leaders were taken out of politics, I think that it would be a great deal better. My husband is a voter; he is a citizen; what taxes we have to pay, we pay; and I think every man that is a taxpayer should have protection.

Q. (*By Mr. Clarke.*) You think your husband would not have any objection to belonging to the union?—A. My husband has never refused to belong to the union, but the conditions were such in the unions that no honorable man could belong to them and keep his respect. When a man belongs to a labor union once he ceases to be a free agent; he loses his individuality; it is what the president or the secretary wishes to do. In the city of Chicago to-day there are hundreds of families suffering for the necessities of life. Is the secretary or the business agent—are their cellars empty? The business agent draws $3 or whatever the standard rate of pay is. Gompers drawing his $9,000 a year—

Q. (*By Mr. Kennedy.*) Who?—A. Gompers. What is his salary?

Mr. Kennedy: Mr. Gompers' salary is $1,500.

The Witness: Mr. Gompers—I give him credit for a great deal of executive ability. To have to work at his trade as a cigar maker, his average at $15 a week, he would not be receiving $1,500 a year. He would not be going to Cuba for his health. His cellars are not empty. His children are not staying home from school for the need of proper clothing.

Mr. Kennedy: From what I know of Mr. Gompers, and I have been at his house in Washington, he lives as ordinarily as any $12 a week man.

The Witness: What does he do with his family?

Mr. Kennedy: He has a very large family, and lives very simply.

The Witness: They have all the comforts of life. Who is O'Connell?

Mr. Kennedy: I do not know him.

The Witness: He is one of them; patent leather shoes and fine clothes. There are hundreds of them. I could mention them by name—officers of different unions; they are not suffering.

20

Finley Peter Dunne: Mr. Dooley on Hens Laying Eggs without the Union Label[1]

Finley Peter Dunne was an authentic comic genius. His parodies of American life before and after the turn of the century remain important social commentaries. The following episode between Mr. Dooley and his straight man "Hennessy" reveals the absurdity of certain union practices and helps us understand the hostile public opinion Gompers (and organized labor) faced. Dunne's sympathy for labor becomes wryly apparent, but his humor expresses the growing frustration of middle-class America.

"I see th' sthrike has been called off," said Mr. Hennessy.

"Which wan?" asked Mr. Dooley. "I can't keep thrack iv thim. Somebody is sthrikin' all th' time. Wan day th' horseshoers are out, an' another day th' teamsters. Th' Brotherhood iv Molasses Candy Pullers sthrikes, an' th' Amalgymated Union iv Pickle Sorters quits in sympathy. Th' carpinter that has been puttin' up a chicken coop f'r Hogan knocked off wurruk whin he found that Hogan was shavin' himsilf without a card fr'm th' Barbers' Union. Hogan fixed it with th' walkin' dillygate iv th' barbers, an' th' carpinter quit wurruk because he found that Hogan was wearin' a pair iv non-union pants. Hogan wint downtown an' had his pants unionized an' come home to find that th' carpinter had sthruck because Hogan's hens was layin' eggs without th' union label. Hogan injooced th' hens to jine th' union. But wan iv thim laid an egg two days in succission an' th' others sthruck, th' rule iv th' union bein' that no hen shall lay more eggs thin th' most reluctant hen in th' bunch.

"It's th' same ivrywhere. I haven't had a sandwich f'r a year because ivry time I've asked f'r wan ayether th' butchers or th' bakers has been out on sthrike. If I go down in a car in th' mornin' it's eight to

[1] From Finley Peter Dunne, "The Labor Troubles," in *Dissertations by Mr. Dooley* (New York, 1906).

wan I walk back at night. A man I knew had his uncle in th' house much longer than ayether iv thim had intinded on account iv a sthrike iv th' Frindly Brotherhood iv Morchuary Helpers. Afther they'd got a permit fr'm th' walkin' dillygate an' th' remains was carrid away undher a profusyon iv floral imblims with a union label on each iv thim, th' coortege was stopped at ivry corner be a picket, who first punched th' mourners an' thin examined their credintials. Me frind says to me: 'Uncle Bill wud've been proud. He was very fond iv long fun'rals, an' this was th' longest I iver attinded. It took eight hours, an' was much more riochous goin' out thin comin' back,' he says.

"It was diff'rent whin I was a young man, Hinnissy. In thim days Capital an' Labor were frindly, or Labor was. Capital was like a father to Labor, givin' it its boord an' lodgin's. Nayether intherfered with th' other. Capital wint on capitalizin', an' Labor wint on laborin'. In thim goolden days a wurrukin' man was an honest artisan. That's what he was proud to be called. Th' week befure iliction he had his pitcher in th' funny pa-apers. He wore a square paper cap an' a leather apron, an' he had his ar-rm ar-round Capital, a rosy binivolint old guy with a plug-hat an' eye-glasses. They were goin' to th' polls together to vote f'r simple old Capital.

"Capital an' Labor walked ar-rm in ar-rm instead iv havin' both hands free as at prisint. Capital was contint to be Capital, an' Labor was used to bein' Labor. Capital come ar-round an' felt th' ar-rm iv Labor wanst in a while, an' ivry year Mrs. Capital called on Mrs. Labor an' congratylated her on her score. Th' pride iv ivry artisan was to wurruk as long at his task as th' boss cud afford to pay th' gas bill. In return f'r his fidelity he got a turkey ivry year. At Chris'mas time Capital gathered his happy fam'ly around him, an' in th' prisince iv th' ladies iv th' neighborhood give thim a short oration. 'Me brave la-ads,' says he, 'we've had a good year. (Cheers.) I have made a millyon dollars. (Sinsation.) I atthribute this to me supeeryor skill, aided be ye'er arnest efforts at th' bench an' at th' forge. (Sobs.) Ye have done so well that we won't need so manny iv us as we did. (Long an' con-tinyous cheerin'.) Those iv us who can do two men's wurruk will remain, an', if possible, do four. Our other faithful sarvants,' he says, 'can come back in th' spring,' he says, 'if alive,' he says. An' th' bold artysans tossed their paper caps in th' air an' give three cheers f'r Capital. They wurruked till ol' age crept on thim, and thin retired to live on th' wish-bones an' kind wurruds they had accumylated.

"Nowadays 'tis far diff'rent. Th' unions has desthroyed all individjool effort. Year be year th' hours iv th' misguided wurrukin' man has been cut down, till now it takes a split-second watch to time him as he goes through th' day's wurruk. I have a gintleman plasthrer frind who tells me he hasn't put in a full day in a year. He goes to his desk ivry mornin' at tin an' sthrikes punchooly at iliven. 'Th' wrongs iv th' wurrukin' men mus' be redhressed,' says he. 'Ar-re ye inthrested in thim?' says I. 'Ye niver looked betther in ye'er life,' says I. 'I niver felt betther,' he says. 'It's th' out-iv-dure life,' he says. 'I haven't missed a baseball game this summer,' he says. 'But,' he says, 'I need exercise. I wish Labor Day wud come around. Th' boys has choose me to carry a life-size model iv th' Masonic Temple in th' parade,' he says.

"If I was a wurrukin' man I'd sigh f'r th' good ol' days, whin Labor an' Capital were frinds. Those who lived through thim did. In thim times th' arrystocracy iv labor was th' la-ads who r-run th' railroad injines. They were a proud race. It was a boast to have wan iv thim in a fam'ly. They niver struck. 'Twas again' their rules. They conferred with Capital. Capital used to weep over thim. Ivry wanst in a while a railroad prisidint wud grow red in th' face an' burst into song about thim. They were a body that th' nation might well be proud iv. If he had a son who asked f'r no betther fate, he wud ask f'r no betther fate f'r him thin to be a Brotherhood iv Locymotive Ingineers. Ivrybody looked up to thim, an' they looked down on ivry-body, but mostly on th' bricklayers. Th' bricklayers were niver bul-warks iv th' constichoochion. They niver conferred with Capital. Th' polis always arrived just as th' conference was beginnin'. Their motto was a long life an' a merry wan: a brick in th' hand is worth two on th' wall. They struck ivry time they thought iv it. They struck on th' slightest provocation, an' whin they weren't provoked at all. If a band wint by they climbed down th' laddhers an' followed it, carryin' banners with th' wurruds: 'Give us bread or we starve,' an' walked till they were almost hungry. Ivry Saturdah night they held a dance to protest again' their wrongs. In th' summer-time th' wails iv th' oppressed bricklayers wint up fr'm countless picnics. They struck in sympathy with annybody. Th' union wint out as wan man because they was a rumor that th' superintindent iv th' rollin'-mills was not nice to his wife. Wanst they struck because Poland was not free.

"What was th' raysult? Their unraisoning demands fin'lly enraged Capital. To-day ye can go into a bricklayer's house an' niver see a capitalist but th' bricklayer himself. Forty years ago a bricklayer was certain iv twelve hours wurruk a day, or two hours more thin a con-victed burglar. To-day he has practically nawthin' to do, an' won't do that. They ar-re out iv wurruk nearly all th' time an' at th' seashore. Jus' as often as ye read 'Newport colony fillin' up,' ye read, 'Bricklayers sthrike again.' Ye very sildom see a bricklayer nowadays in th' city. They live mostly in th' counthry, an' on'y come into town to be bribed to go to wurruk. It wud pay anny man who is buildin' a house to sind thim what money he has be mail an' go live in a tent.

"An' all this time, how about th' arrystocracy iv labor, th' knights iv th' throttle? Have they been deprived iv anny hours iv labor? On th' conthry, they have steadily increased, ontil to-day there is not a knight iv th' throttle who hasn't more hours iv wurruk in a day thin he can use in a week. In th' arly mornin', whin he takes his ir'n horse out iv th' stall, he meets th' onforchnit, misguided bricklayer comin' home in a cab fr'm a sthrike meetin'. Hardly a year passes that he can't say to his wife: 'Mother, I've had an increase.' 'In wages?' 'No, in hours.' It's th' old story iv th' ant an' th' grasshopper—th' ant that ye can step on an' th' grasshopper ye can't catch.

"Well, it's too bad that th' goolden days has passed, Hinnissy. Capital still pats Labor on th' back, but on'y with an axe. Labor rayfuses to be treated as a frind. It wants to be treated as an inimy. It thinks it gets more that way. They ar-re still a happy fam'ly, but it's more like an English fam'ly. They don't speak. What do I think iv it all? Ah, sure, I don't know. I belong to th' onforchnit middle class. I wurruk hard, an' I have no money. They come in here undher me hospital roof, an' I furnish thim with cards, checks, an' refreshmints. 'Let's play without a limit,' says Labor. 'It's Dooley's money.' 'Go as far as ye like with Dooley's money,' says Capital. 'What have ye got?' 'I've got a straight to Roosevelt,' says Labor. 'I've got ye beat,' says Capital. 'I've got a Supreme Court full of injunctions.' Manetime I've pawned me watch to pay f'r th' game, an' I have to go to th' joolry-store on th' corner to buy a pound iv beef or a scuttle iv coal. No wan iver strikes in sympathy with me."

"They ought to get together," said Mr. Hennessy.

"How cud they get anny closer together thin their prisint clinch?" asked Mr. Dooley. "They're so close together now that those that ar-re between thim ar-re crushed to death."

21

John Kirby, Jr.: Injunctions Are Necessary (1904)[1]

> *The campaign to stop government injunctions against striking unions centered on the Peare Anti-Injunction Bill introduced in the House in 1904. Extensive hearings were held but the bill never passed. The political program of the AFL, launched in 1906, demanded passage of the bill as the key to labor's political and economic hopes. The following statement by a very conservative manufacturer from Ohio is a militant example of opposition to Gompers from the Right. Kirby was active in the National Association of Manufacturers.*

I come representing the Employers' Association of Dayton, Ohio, which is an organization composed of the employers of that city, and includes the various local trades associations.

I also represent the Citizens' Industrial Association of America; also, the Citizens' Industrial Association of Dayton, an organization composed principally of workingmen, but which includes professional and business men in its membership. I also represent the National Association of Manufacturers and the National Metal Trades Association, and in addition to these organizations I shall speak in the interest of all citizens of this country who believe in the perpetuity of its government and the principles upon which it is founded. I shall speak for the maintenance of those inalienable rights which the Constitution of the United States declares shall be enjoyed by its every citizen, and I shall appeal to you as the representatives of the institutions under which our citizens have prospered as have no other people on earth, to not report favorably upon that specious but insidious Gompers-Mitchell anti-injunction bill which you have in your keeping, with the power to so emphatically condemn that it shall, for a long time to come, be a warning to its promoters and advocates to not pester the people's representatives with attempts to formulate such pernicious legislation as this bill represents.

[1] From Hearings, Anti-Injunction [Peare] Bill, House Judiciary Committee, March 22, 1904 (Washington, D. C., 1904), pp. 681–95.

The record of organized labor is so stained with injustice and crime that it would seem unnecessary that I should refer to any specific instances in support of my opposition to the measure under consideration here, and which has for several years absorbed the time and attention of the Judiciary Committees of the House and Senate of the United States.

I come to you not as a lawyer, not as a capitalist, not as an orator, but as a man who has rubbed up against the hard side of life, having fought its battles ever since I was 12 years of age. I have been a working boy, and I come before you to-day as a workingman; not, however, as an eight-hour day, anti-injunction, union-label workingman, but as a representative of the class of workingmen who believe in the principles set forth in the bill of rights; who believe in and are loyal to this Government, and who foster and encourage our police, our militia, and other systems which are established to safeguard its institutions.

John Mitchell is quoted as saying, "The American wage-earner has made up his mind that he must always remain a wage-earner." If the statement is intended as general, as it appears to be, I say it is basely false and without foundation or justification, and that no man free from the fallacies of socialism and the despotism of anarchy, when protected in his rights of citizenship (especially in view of the thousands upon thousands of our men of affairs of to-day who were the laborers of yesterday), will of his own free will subscribe to any such doctrine or will to his heirs such a shameful inheritance; and if you, gentlemen of this committee, will by your unanimous vote relegate that anti-injunction bill to where it belongs it will not longer trouble the substantial and loyal citizens of this country as it has troubled them in the past and is now troubling them. Moreover, you will remove a great load from the minds of millions of ambitious and hopeful wage-earners of this country who see in the enactment into law of such a bill the erection of a great barrier to their energies, if not an entirely hopeless future for opportunity to ever become anything more than what Mr. Mitchell says they have already made up their minds to be.

For years we have heard the cry of "Workingmen, strike against government by injunction!" but from whom does it come? Does that cry come from the men who respect and obey the laws? Not by any means. It comes from the followers of Sam Parks. It comes from the element that expelled William Potter from the union because he obeyed the order of Governor Odell and served with the militia in suppressing the riotous mob which was destroying the property of the Hudson Valley Railway Company in the name of organized labor; the element which makes a member of our State militia ineligible to its union membership; the element which in cases of labor strikes at once proceeds to cripple the police and paralyze the arm of the law. It comes from the element of organized labor which frowns upon government of any form which opposes the use of brass knuckles and brickbats as a means of inducing free men to join the ranks of organized slavery. It comes from the element represented by the third vice-president of the Machinists' International Union, who closed his annual report for 1903 by referring to the strike on the Union Pacific Railroad in these words:

> I wish to say that this climate is not conducive to the health of scabs, as quite a few of them have been sent back home quite ill.

And from the elment represented by the fourth vice-president of the same union, who, referring to the same strike, in his annual report said:

> The hospitals are full of scabs that have got hurt at work and in fights between themselves. Four have died at Cheyenne and one was killed at Omaha in a fight, while three or four others have been killed in the shop. The picket duty is done in a very systematic manner, and we are keeping tab on the scabs day and night. There is not a scab on the line that is not known to us now. The professionals are the only ones that stay, and you can do only one thing with them.

It comes from the Hay Market element of Chicago. It comes from the element which proposes that the youth of this country shall grow up common street loafers or tramps instead of useful and industrious citizens, and from that element of society which seeks to either rule or tear down and destroy the things which by perseverance and energy the industrious have built up. Gentlemen of the committee, I submit for your consideration the question, Does it come from the law-abiding workingmen of America?

Mr. Gompers has spoken to you in support of this bill. His chief argument appears to be that organized labor is made the exception in the administration and execution of the law, and therein I fully agree with him, for I know from my own experience that it has been a most difficult matter to obtain conviction of a member of a labor union for a crime committed in the interest of organized labor.

I will not take up your time by a lengthy answer to what Mr. Gompers had to say in support of the bill; but I want to call your attention to the manner in which he exerts his influence to have his constituents obey the law and respect our courts, as indicated in an address at a meeting of the striking cigar makers a few years ago in New York, and in which he was quoted in the Associated Press reports as saying:

Never in the history of the world has a tyrant been found without a judge to clothe his tyranny in the form of law, and a fitting representative of this class is found in a judge who by his actions belies his own name, for he is called Freedman. I am here especially to violate the injunction. I have done so before at a distance, and now I want to face the music if there is any.

Will the promoters of this measure tell us in what manner any citizen, be his occupation what is may, is injured by the writ of injunction as it relates to labor disputes? Can they show that it does more than to interfere with their rule or ruin policy, and is it not as plain as the nose on a man's face that it is because of this interference that they want it removed? Does not Gompers's argument, when boiled down to its logical conclusions, admit this? If not, then why did he object to the amendment, "not involving injury to property or breach of peace?"

Mr. Gompers said to you, "As a final result the men struck work, and they were served with injunctions," and in justification of his support he cites a number of petitions upon which injunctions were granted, and proposes as a remedy the removal of one of the most important safeguards of the law. What were those men enjoined from doing, and what of the consequences if those injunctions could not have been granted? I would like to ask my friend and neighbor, Mr. Nevin, who is a member of this committee, what the consequences to me and the manufacturing plant of which I have charge would have been had we been deprived of that, the only protection left to us. And whom did it injure? Mr. Gompers says the courts have exceeded their authority, and proposes as a panacea for the ills of which he complains that the patient be cured by killing it; that the authority of the courts be taken away, and that the interests of employers, employees, and the great public be left to the tender mercies of the equity court of organized labor. What a beautiful mess we would be in, wouldn't we?

Mr. Gompers says injunctions do not reach rioters and lawbreakers. If this be true, then why is it that rioters and lawbreakers detest them as they do and cry so long and loud against "government by injunction"? As a matter of fact there is no branch of the law that rioters and lawbreakers fear so much as the writ of injunction, proof whereof lies in the strenuous efforts they are making to have it removed.

Gentleman, I say to you this effort on the part of organized labor to scatter to the winds an institution of law which has stood for ages as the safeguard of the people against irreparable loss and injury is at war with every principle of peace and justice. It is a species of anarchy, for its purpose is none other than to pave the way for mob rule and injustice. Picture in your minds the utter helplessness of the employers and nonunion men of this country with this protecting arm of the court withdrawn from their support, and draw your conclusions as to the effect of such a condition upon our manufacturing and commercial industries; for it the Federal Government should pass such a law it would be but a brief time until the State legislatures, under the same pressure, would follow suit.

Mr. Gompers has called your attention to the joint conference of mine operators and miners held at Indianapolis recently. This conference resulted in a failure to agree and a strike of the miners was threatened. The operators made a proposition which the miners' representatives refused to accept. The question was put to a vote of all the miners interested in the conference and, fortunately for the country, they voted in favor of accepting the proposition made by the operators. Nevertheless, pending the result of that vote, the operators and the great public were trembling with fear lest the action of those representatives might be sustained and a strike follow. And why? Simply because they believed that in event of a strike history would repeat itself, and that a strike meant a repetition of the acts of lawlessness and crime which were perpetrated during the anthracite coal strike of 1902 and the more recent experience in the mining regions of the West. And what good citizen, I ask, would withhold from our courts the power to forestall such a reign of anarchy as existed in those coal regions as a result of those strikes?

Mr. Gompers has talked to you about criminal law by which crime can be punished, but he said nothing about the difficulties which in labor strikes are always encountered in attempts to administer it, nor did he say to what extent he, as the head representative of the element which causes so much turbulence and commits so much crime, has used his official position to suppress it or bring the perpetrators to justice. I will ask him where, when, and how often members of his constituent organizations who have been convicted of crime have been expelled, or even disciplined, by the union for it? Those urging the bill know full well the impracticability of individual prosecution, in most of such cases, for malicious injury, because of the barrier which the secrecy and obligations of the unions present to the procurement of convicting testimony, and the difficulty in procuring juries to convict. "By their fruits ye shall know them."

Mr. Gompers has said to you:

> I do not pretend to say that here and there you will not find some crack-brained, irresponsible, and, perhaps, some faithless men.

"Here and there." What modesty! I would like to know what strike of any consequence has taken place in this country, where the employer attempted to run his business with other men, where these "crack-brained irresponsibles" have not bobbed up with brass knuckles, brickbats, and dynamite in sufficient numbers to paralyze the whole community, and in all, or nearly all, cases of prosecution they are defended by the lawyers and funds of the unions of which Mr. Gompers is the responsible head.

Do not be deceived, gentlemen, by the sophistry of the men who are making a business and drawing salaries and levying graft upon the victims of this pernicious thing which is breeding socialism and anarchy in our midst. It is the duty of every well-disposed and patriotic American citizen to look this evil squarely in the face and perform his full duty in the premises, as I trust and believe you will do. It is the perpetrators and endorsers of such deeds as those who are nagging you to act favorably upon that bill. Will you do it? I don't believe you will.

22
Politician

The publication of the AFL political demands in 1906 was followed by an intensive campaign against labor's enemies. Maine's traditionally early election in September provided Gompers with an ideal opportunity to defeat a powerful antilabor House member, Charles Littlefield. Theodore Roosevelt sent Albert Beveridge, Speaker of the House "Uncle Joe" Cannon, William Howard Taft, and a phalanx of party stalwarts to help Littlefield. If Gompers could defeat Littlefield in September, then the November national congressional election might turn on labor's political influence. Nevertheless, Littlefield won, although his victory margin was greatly reduced. But all of Maine's Republican congressmen were reelected with reduced majorities due to a Prohibition party campaign. After Littlefield's victory, Gompers tried to defeat Cannon in his Illinois home district. Later, during the 1908 presidential campaign, he ardently supported Bryan against Taft.

CANNON TO THEODORE ROOSEVELT (1906)[1]

Like all other great associations, [the AFL] numbers among its members perhaps sometimes foolish men and sometimes selfish men who seek to mislead it. In my judgement, those men who, under the lead of Mr. Gompers, seek the enactment of class legislation and propose to blacklist all who do not assent to their demand, are the worst enemies that organized labor can have." RR men are the best workers. I am glad that the railway organizations are not federated under the leadership of Mr. Gompers. It seems to me Mr. Gompers makes his principal fight upon you, as you are leader of the party; but, instead of making this feature prominent and hurling his abuse directly at you, he seeks to reach your administration by attacking those of us who have not the same strength that you have, notably Taft, Littlefield, myself, and various others. If Mr. Gompers puts forty or fifty of his working force into my district, where, I suppose, there are from

[1] September 14, 1906. Papers of Theodore Roosevelt, Library of Congress.

four to five thousand voters who belong to the Federation of Labor, I may be compelled to spend the last week in my district. [But] I do not fear Mr. Gompers. . . . Mitchell could cause him more trouble than SG because of coal miners in district. Pleased about Maine campaign.

"UNCLE JOE" CANNON ON GOMPERS' POLITICS (1906)[2]

The Republican party is a labor party. South of an imaginary line labor was owned. North of that line, free men and sovereigns did the labor. The War came and Slavery ended. Now it was free labor, North and South. I said we were a party of labor. WE were so organized, and that was our first work.

I want to say that Mr. Littlefield is as good as we have in the 386 members. Do I agree with Littlefield on all matters?

No. Littlefield, like the tall pine, 6 feet, 4 inches, physically and 6 feet, 4 inches, mentally and intellectually is uncommonly uncomfortable at times. But President Theodore Roosevelt favored his support of Littlefield. Taft is going down there too. Littlefield is the first man on the black list. Samuel Gompers has come into your district and demanded the defeat of Littlefield, not because Littlefield has failed to properly represent the district or even the workingmen here, but because he has failed to comply with the demands of Mr. Gompers who claims to be a citizen of New York and a resident of Washington. Mr. Gompers has introduced a new element into American politics. He does not exercise the right of petition, he demands that Congress enact into law his will. He does not appeal to you, he commands you if you are a member of the Federation to go to the polls and vote as he would vote. He does not come here to argue, he publishes a decree in the name of labor that the public official who refused to obey his command shall be retired from public life.

On what meat does this new Caesar feed to make him different from other political bosses in this day of the decadence of bossism?

I do not believe in proscription in politics. It is foreign to our institutions, foreign to a government of the people.

A member of the [AFL] may be a Republican in favor of Republican policies but he is assessed to make a campaign against his own interest as he sees them because Mr. Gompers is opposed. Methods like these never succeed in the United States. The old Know-Nothing party tried this method of blacklisting all who were not native born. It would have blacklisted Mr. Gompers and other Federation leaders as not

[2] Lewiston (Maine) *Daily Sun,* September 6, 1906.

qualified to hold public office. But the life of that party was short. I remember when demagogues, not farmers, but demagogues tried to form the farmers into an alliance to secure exceptional legislation not given to other citizens. It failed because farmers stampeded it to death. The farmers are more than one-third of the people but they ask no legislation that is not general to all the people.

Every man is a "co-sovereign" and he exercises his inalienable right to unite with his fellows—farmers, doctors, lawyers, etc.—to persue policies which are the best for the whole people. Workers are jealous of this sovereignty and they will work under their own hat brims and not under that of Mr. Gompers.

Samuel Gompers' grievances are unconstitutional and unfair. He attacks Theodore Roosevelt and Littlefield and 40 or 50 other men in public life. He has read us out of civilization. But I would rather retire now than compromise the law or civilization. Laboring men should put their feet upon Mr. Gompers' proposition because it is unrepublican, undemocratic, un-American.

WILLIAM HOWARD TAFT TO THEODORE ROOSEVELT (1908) [3]

Your letter with respect to Bryan and Gompers was not so much directed to labor as it was to people who ought to be thoroughly stirred up in respect to what they may look for, should Bryan and Gompers get into power, with respect to the courts and the interference with their processes. In one aspect I think that it is the most important issue of the campaign, and I am sure that the Gompers letter will stir up a great many people who had been rather apathetic.

In respect to the labor defection . . . every once in a while I get up in the morning with a cold sweat, because that puts such a new phase on the situation and one so different from what we have had in past campaigns that it may be difficult to calculate what it is. Still labor is ordinarily not quiet in its declarations, and Gompers and his other bazoo players have been attempting to arouse all laborers to declarations so that perhaps we have heard all there is.

ELECTION OF 1908–10

When a man like John Mitchell advises the workingmen to sustain Gompers and vote for Bryan, is there any earthly reason why workingmen should listen to Joe Cannon who reviles Gompers and organized labor? [4]

[3] November 1, 1908. Papers of Theodore Roosevelt, Library of Congress.
[4] York, Pennsylvania *Gazette*, October 3, 1908.

Samuel Gompers' reelection as President of the A.F.L. must be interpreted as signifying that one of the lessons of the election was lost upon the [Federation]. Bryan made the injunction issue one of his headliners. Mr. Gompers exalted it into the Hamlet of his political play. At the polls, injunctions were victorious and . . . will persist. It is somewhat superfluous to add, so will Mr. Gompers. [Quoting Knights of Labor *Journal* with approval: "Gompers, Mitchell and Morrison should know that the spirit of Czolgosz[5] does not sway good men"].[6]

Union laborers are mostly Republicans and the broadest coquetery on the part of the Democracy, supplemented by Samuel Gompers and his friends, has not sufficed to win a large number of them from their allegiance to the Republicans. The average American citizen seems to be instinctively averse to making himself merely one of a herd.[7]

[5] Anarchist and assassin of President William McKinley (1901).
[6] *Brooklyn Daily Eagle*, December 18, 1908.
[7] Galveston (Texas) *News*, May 7, 1910.

23
Headed for Prison (1908)

The following excerpts are drawn from newspaper comments published after Judge Wright sentenced Gompers and two other union officials for contempt of court, the main issue following the Bucks Stove case.

The *Sun* says:

Gompers has only suffered the fate that has overtaken and submerged all who have associated themselves with Roosevelt in promotion of his political and economic policies. One after another they have fallen from the heights of favor to the lowest depths of unpropitious circumstances. The same road has been travelled by a numerous and notable body of citizens whose stomachs revolted or whose usefulness ended, and who in consequence experienced the most remarkable and interesting decline in desirability. Well may Gompers rail at unkind fate. "Twelve months in jail for me, for Mitchell nine months, six months for poor Morrison. For our honored and fortunate accomplice, two years in Africa."

The *Times* says:

Event shows that it was not pure bravado for Gompers to declare that he was going to Washington to jail, if it were necessary. It appears both that it is necessary and that Gompers has made serious mistakes in the time and manner of going to jail. Who knows how many votes it would have been worth for him to have received his sentence before election. If he had edited the *Federationist* from his cell his martyrdom might have been worth while, but now he gets a year on the same day that he affronts a great and good friend who alone might have lightened the weight of his sentence. Surely it was a mistake yesterday to charge the President with "villification."

The court referred to the use of the "We don't patronize" list and "Unfair" list of the labor organization and said that members of labor unions were forced and coerced into supporting it "whether individually willing or unwilling, approving or disapproving," by various methods.

With tears coursing down his cheeks, Gompers heard the order of the court which condemned him to prison for a year. Both Mitchell and Morrison seemed stunned, although Mitchell appeared to be the less concerned. Asked if he had anything to say why sentence should not be pronounced, President Gompers declared that he had not consciously violated any law.

The decision of Justice Wright, which consumed two hours and twenty minutes in reading, was one of the most scathing arraignments that ever came from the Bench in this city. "Everywhere," the court said, "all over, within the court and out, utter, rampant, insolent defiance is heralded and proclaimed; unrefined insult, coarse affront, vulgar indignity, measure the litigant's conception of the tribunal wherein his cause still pends."

Whether President Roosevelt will take any action, as he had been urged to do in telegrams received from different labor organizations throughout the country, in connection with Judge Wright's decision, has not been decided. . . .

The *American* says:

> Assuming from the language of Judge Wright that the decision is based in great part on Sherman's anti-trust law, we do not believe that the majority of fair-minded men of the country will approve the sentence of the district court. The courts are habitually sending labor men to jail, not for crimes, but for infractions of rules laid down under the authority of this law. Trust magnates do the same things that labor leaders do, but they are not sent to jail. When trust magnates are convicted, they are fined, but the labor man is jailed. While these decisions may be within the law they are enforced with great inequality.

The *World* says:

> The reasons why these men ought to be punished should be stated without passion, or intemperate language, or denunciatory epithet. The labor leaders will be able to cite words and expressions from Judge Wright's decision with which to persuade their followers that the court was prejudiced against all labor unions. . . .

The various labor unions in protesting to the President against the sentence, urge him to prevent the incarceration of the labor leaders. The Illinois United Mine Workers' sent this telegram, signed by President John H. Walker, the vice-president, secretary-treasurer, and members of the executive board:

> In the name of 75,000 mine workers in Illinois, we desire to protest against the decision committing to penal servitude those great com-

moners and representatives of American labor movements, Samuel Gompers, John Mitchell, and Frank Morrison. These men may be guilty of a breach of law, but a law that denies the use of a free press and full speech is a breach of the fundamental principles of our country. Such decisions only tend to create enmity and class hatred. We respectfully solicit your influence to prevent the incarceration of these men.

The Judge's Denunciation

Judge Wright's decision was a scathing denunciation of the defendants. He recited the conditions anteceding the injunction and referred to the fact that for twenty-five years the Bucks plant had operated a ten-hour shop, and always had maintained an open shop. He also spoke of the numerical strength of the American Federation of Labor, with its 2,000,000 members, and of its repeated endorsement of the boycott of the Bucks Stove and Range Company, through the *American Federationist,* the Federation's official organ, speeches by the defendants, letters, circulars, etc. The court referred to the use of the "we don't patronize" list and "unfair" list of the labor organizations, and said that members of labor unions were forced and coerced into supporting it "whether individually willing or unwilling, approving or disapproving," by various methods.

The court read extracts from numbers of resolutions of labor organizations bearing on the Bucks case, as tending to show the methods of influencing members of unions. "And these methods," the court remarked, "seem to be known as persuasion." **. . .**

What Combination Was

Following an exhaustive discussion of the conspiracies in restraint of trade, Judge Wright said:

> From the foregoing it ought to seem apparent to thoughtful men that the defendants to the bill, each and all of them, have combined together for the purpose of:
> 1—Bringing about the breach of plaintiff's existing contracts with others.
> 2—Depriving plaintiff of property (the value of the good-will of its business) without due process of law.
> 3—Restraining trade among the several states.
> 4—Restraining commerce among the several states.

The ultimate purpose of the defendants, said the court, in this connection was unlawful, their concerted project an offence against the law, and, it added, they were guilty of crime.

Complicity of the Accused

Regarding the violation of the court's injunction, Justice Wright said:—

> That Gompers and others had in advance of the injunction determined to violate it if issued, and had in advance of the injunction counselled all members of the labor unions and of the American Federation of Labor and the public generally to violate it in case it should be issued, appears from the following. . . .

The court here read a mass of extracts from reports of proceedings of the Federation, reports of President Gompers, editorials from the American Federationist and the labor press generally.

As to Secretary Frank Morrison, the court declared that he had full knowledge of all that was being done, taking part in the preparation and publication of the American Federationist of April, 1908.

Concerning Mitchell, the court pointed to various acts by him which, he said, placed him within the pale of the law.

He quoted from Mitchell's book on "Organized Labor" certain passages wherein Mitchell declared that it was the duty of all patriotic and law-abiding citizens to resist or disregard injunctions when they forbid the doing of a thing which is lawful. Mitchell also was credited with signing, "with full knowledge, the urgent appeal which accompanied the twenty-seven thousand or more circular letters to the various labor union secretaries and with full knowledge of their contents, counselling their distribution and with the same purpose and intent." The court also referred to the presence of Mitchell in the chair on January 25, 1908, at the annual convention of the United Mine Workers of America, when a resolution was adopted placing the Bucks Stove and Range Company on the "unfair list."

Continuing, the court said:

> In defence of the charges now at bar no defence is offered save these: "That the injunction (1) infringed the constitutional guaranty of freedom of the press, and (2) infringed the constitution guaranty of freedom of speech."
>
> The injunction interferes with no legitimate right of criticism or comment that the law has ever sanctioned and the respondents' intimation that it does so is a mockery and a pretense.

In reference to the freedom of the press, the court declared that the constitution nowhere conferred the right to speak, to print or to publish. "It guarantees," said he, "only that in so far as the Federal

Government is concerned its congress shall not abridge it and leaves the subject to the regulation of the several states, where it belongs."

"No right," the court added, "to publish the libel or the slander can be sustained, except upon theory of a right to do wrong."

Opinions on Judgment

Detroit, December 24

"I think you will find that Mr. Gompers, Mr. Mitchell, and Mr. Morrison will never serve their sentences," was the comment Commissioner General of Immigration Daniel J. Keefe, former vice-president of the American Federation of Labor and head of the Longshoremen's Union, made regarding today's decision in the Bucks Stove Company case.

Indianapolis, Ind., December 24

W. D. Ryan, national secretary-treasurer of the United Mine Workers of which John Mitchell was president, when the alleged boycott resolution was acted upon, at the miner's convention a year ago, sent the following telegram to President Roosevelt:

> As an official representative of the United States Mine Workers of America, I emphatically protest against the court decision sending Gompers, Mitchell and Morrison to jail. I know of the law that has been violated by Gompers or Morrison in connection with the case in question, and I am positively certain that Mitchell is absolutely innocent.

Philadelphia, December 24

James M. Beck, of New York, counsel for the Bucks Stove Company, when informed of the decision in the labor case at Washington, while in this city yesterday, said:

> This case ought to be the death-knell of the boycott. If so, it is the most important decision in a labor controversy since the Debs case, of 1906, from which it differs only in the fact that in the Debs case physical violence was used to paralyze interstate traffic. In the Bucks Stove case, the insidious and far more dangerous method of a national boycott was employed.

Boston, December 24

First vice-president James Duncan, of the American Federation of Labor, said last night:

> I am of the opinion that the pardoning power of the President could be used right away in causing the release of President Gompers.

If President Gompers is compelled to spend the year's term in jail, he will conduct the affairs of the Federation in the jail in which he is confined.

I think the decision is the most unjust that I have ever heard.

Other labor leaders, including President John F. Tobin, of the Boot and Shoe Workers' Union, expressed similar disapproval of the decision.

24

V. I. Lenin: Working-Class Aristocrat[1]

The founding father of the Bolsheviks and the Russian Revolution, V. I. Lenin had little use for Gompers or his labor philosophy. Before the revolution he considered Gompers a mere class collaborator; after the revolution, he called Gompers a "social traitor" for supporting America's role in World War I and for refusing to aid the struggling Soviet cause. Lenin was a close and shrewd student of American economic development, and a number of his insights into American race and labor policies remain peculiarly relevant today.

The 32nd Annual Convention of the American Federation of Labour, as the association of trade unions is called, has come to a close in Rochester. Alongside the rapidly growing Socialist Party, this association is a living relic of the past: of the old craft-union, liberal-bourgeois traditions that hang full weight over America's working-class *aristocracy.*

On August 31, 1911, the Federation had 1,841,268 members. Samuel Gompers, a strong opponent of socialism, was re-elected President. But Max Hayes, the socialist workers' candidate, received 5,074 votes against Gompers's 11,974, whereas previously Gompers used to be elected unanimously. The struggle of the socialists against the "trade unionists" in the American trade union movement is slowly but surely leading to the victory of the former over the latter.

Gompers not only fully accepts the bourgeois myth of "harmony between labour and capital," but carries on a downright bourgeois policy in the Federation against the socialist one, although he professes to stand for the complete political "neutrality" of the trade unions! During the recent presidential elections in America, Gompers reprinted in the Federation's official publication the programmes and platforms of all three bourgeois parties (Democrats, Republicans and

[1] From *Lenin on the United States* (New York: International Publishers Co., Inc., 1970), pp. 56–57.

Progressists) but did *not* reprint the programme of the *Socialist* Party!!

Protests against this mode of action were voiced at the Rochester Convention even by Gompers's own followers.

The state of affairs in the American labour movement shows us, as it does in Britain, the remarkably clear-cut division between purely trade unionist and socialist strivings, the split between *bourgeois labour policy* and socialist labour policy. For, strange as it may seem, in capitalist society even the working class can carry on a bourgeois policy, if it forgets about its emancipatory aims, puts up with wage-slavery and confines itself to seeking alliances now with one bourgeois party, now with another, for the sake of imaginary "improvements" in its indentured condition.

The principal historical cause of the particular prominence and (temporary) strength of bourgeois labour policy in Britain and America is the long-standing political liberty and the exceptionally favourable conditions, in comparison with other countries, for the deep-going and widespread development of capitalism. These conditions have tended to produce within the working class an aristocracy that has trailed after the bourgeoisie, *betraying* its own class.

In the twentieth century, this peculiar situation in Britain and America is rapidly disappearing. Other countries are catching up with Anglo-Saxon capitalism, and the *mass* of workers are learning about socialism at first hand. The faster the growth of world capitalism, the sooner will socialism triumph in America and Britain.

25

Mr. Gompers
and Dynamite (1911)[1]

*The McNamara case of 1911 caused organized labor
and Gompers great embarrassment. Louis Adamic implies that
Gompers tacitly accepted the use of dynamite and terror in labor
disputes, and that, therefore, he knew the McNamaras plotted to
blow up the Los Angeles* Times *building. "The intrigues that
center about a big labor leader's* [i.e., *Gompers'*] *desk," Adamic
wrote, "are as underhanded and perilous as those which make the
life of the average Prime Minister in the Balkans the thrilling
experience it is."*

Once in jail, the McNamaras became of minor importance as
individuals. The important thing now was the McNamara Case—the
Case of Capitalism *vs.* Labor. The prisoners became symbols of Labor's Struggle—Martyrs—Victims of Capitalist Greed. The case became a National Issue.

Immediately, throughout the country labor leaders and radicals
raised a yell: "Frame-up! Fiendish plot!" Debs telegraphed to the
Appeal to Reason:

> Sound the alarm to the working class! There is to be a repetition
> of the Moyer-Haywood-Pettibone outrage upon the labor movement.
> The secret arrest of John McNamara, by a corporation detective agency,
> has all the earmarks of another conspiracy to fasten the crime of mur-
> der on the labor union officials to discredit and destroy organized labor
> in the United States. . . . Arouse, ye hosts of labor, and swear that the
> villainous plot shall not be consummated! Be not deceived by the
> capitalist press!

Other radicals and laborites likewise declared that the arrests and
the kidnaping were a "frame-up"; among them was O. A. Tveitmoe,

[1] From Louis Adamic, *Dynamite* (New York: Harper & Row, Publishers, Inc.,
1931), pp. 216–17, 236–40. Copyright, 1931, 1934, by Louis Adamic. Copyright ©
renewed 1958 by Stella Adamic. Reprinted by permission of the publisher.

of San Francisco, who, as secretary of the California Building Trades Council, offered a $7000 reward for the apprehension of the person or persons really responsible for the destruction of the Times Building and the killing of twenty men.

Gompers raged:

> I have investigated the entire case. . . . Burns has lied. . . . The whole affair smacks of well-laid pre-arrangement. The interests of corporate wealth are always trying to crush the labor movement, and they use the best way to strike at the men having the confidence of the working people. . . . I admit that we can't compete with the capitalists in questions of litigation. But we will meet them this time on their ground and fight them in their own way, but it is the last time we will do it. There may come a time when we can't meet them that way any more, and when they hang a few of us we will show them a new way to meet an issue.

The San Francisco *Argonaut* remarked:

> And what does Mr. Gompers mean by a "new way"? Surely he can't mean more dynamite, for that is a lamentably old way. There is no novelty about dynamite. . . . It seems that Mr. Gompers protests too much.

On July 27, 1911, the A. F. of L. issued an official appeal to the working class of America to stand by the McNamaras, innocent victims of capitalist greed.

> Funds must be provided to ensure a proper defense, a fair and impartial trial. Eminent counsel have been engaged. In the name of justice and humanity all members of our organization and all friends of justice are urgently requested to contribute. . . .

Gompers received the news of the confessions while returning from the convention in Atlanta.

"I have been grossly imposed upon!" he exclaimed and began to shed tears. "It won't do the labor movement any good!" he blubbered.

In New York City Gompers stopped at the Hotel Victoria. He was interviewed by the New York *Times*—and during the interview there stood or sat around him O. A. Tveitmoe, of San Francisco, and the latter's lieutenant, Anton Johannsen, and other strong-arm men from the Coast who had also attended the Atlanta convention.

Gompers looked haggard; he had not slept for nights. There is no doubt that he had had word of what was coming from his personal representative, "Big Ed" Nockles, in Los Angeles. (Anton Johannsen, whom I saw during the writing of this book, said to me: "Gompers talked and acted all right. I was there with 'im.")

"Can you explain how it happens that you were kept in ignorance?" the reporter asked Gompers.

Gompers: "Explain? Kept in ignorance? Why, we want to know that ourselves. We, who were willing to give our encouragement, our pennies, our faith, why were we not told the truth from the beginning? We had a right to know."

Tveitmoe and Johannsen solemnly nodded their heads, in support of the A. F. of L. chief's indignation.

"We had a right to know," repeated Gompers.

"Do you blame the men in charge of the case for not setting you straight?" he was asked.

Gompers shook his head. "Am I in any position to blame till I know more of what happened?"

"Well, are you in a position to say what would have been your advice if they had sought it on the question of the McNamaras' pleading guilty?"

Gompers's tear-washed face became self-righteously stern. "I would have told them to plead guilty, sir. If they were guilty, if they did this thing, and if they had told me so, I would have said to them to plead guilty. I believe in truth. I believe in candor. I do not believe in violence. Labor does not need violence."

"What will be the attitude of the American Federation of Labor?" the *Times* asked him.

"There will be no particular attitude taken by the Federation," Gompers replied. "If they are guilty, then that ends the case for us, our connection with it. There is nothing more to say except to repeat that we have been cruelly deceived."

But Burns, not a single one of whose statements in connection with the case, as it happens, has yet been proved untrue or inaccurate, said that Gompers had known right along—"from the beginning"—that the McNamaras were guilty.

Reporters asked Burns what he thought of Gompers.

"Why, boys," said Burns, "what I think of that man is unfit to print. Had Gompers been honest, he would have demonstrated it by apologizing, not to me—but to organized labor and the American people generally for his abuse and vilification of me when I arrested the McNamaras. If Gompers is arrested on his contempt charge [in the Buck[s] Stove and Range Company boycott case] now pending against him in Washington, it will be to the interest of labor—decent labor—to lock him up and throw away the key. Gompers cried that the kidnaping of labor leaders by Burns would have to stop. Did he ever open his mouth about stopping murdering men like rats in a trap? Gompers said that the McNamaras and Darrow deceived him. The truth is that Gompers did the deceiving."

Of course, under the circumstances, no one could reasonably have expected Gompers to act differently.

Like their chief, trade-union leaders the country over were "shocked" by the confession. They were "stunned" and "pained," and they denounced the McNamaras and "abhorred their crime." John Mitchell was "astounded" and Frank Morrison was "simply thunderstruck." Separate unions and central labor councils in numerous cities and towns passed resolutions, which they sent to the district attorney and the judge in the case in Los Angeles, urging them to "show no mercy" to the dynamiters, to "give them the limit," "the full penalty of the law."

Burns remarked that some of the leaders denouncing the Mc-Namaras were sincere, others—"most of them"—were not.

Tens of thousands of people throughout the country believed that the men had confessed "to save Darrow from going to prison." Thousands believed—some still do—that they were not guilty at all, but that they had sacrified themselves for Darrow; which, of course, is absurd on the face of it.

Meantime Burns and the United States Department of Justice agents were working on other dynamite cases. "We're going after the men back of the McNamaras," said Burns. "When Gompers says he was deceived, he is uttering a lot of drivel and buncombe."

The conservative press of the entire United States turned upon Gompers and other leaders of the labor movement, upon Darrow, upon the Socialists. Said the New York *Tribune*:

> Mr. Samuel Gompers wept when he heard of the confession. The precise cause of his grief is left to speculation. Perhaps no injustice will be done in assuming that it was more subjective than objective. He probably wept more for his own distress and that of the close corporation which he arrogantly calls "labor" than for the fate of those two friends of his whom he was only yesterday commiserating as the victims of a hellish conspiracy and whom he was quite prepared tomorrow to mourn as holy martyrs.

The *Wall Street Journal* was delighted with Gompers's predicament:

> Doubtless the trusts bribed the McNamaras to confess in order to discredit labor. . . . Mr. Gompers seems almost too good to be true. He has managed to reach the highest position in labor politics while preserving a pristine innocence of mind beside which the newborn

babe seems wallowing in original sin. This good man was moved to tears when he heard [the news]. He never suspected it was coming, although others with inferior sources of information had ample notice. . . . No one short of a congenital idiot could have ascribed [the numerous dynamitings between 1905 and 1910] to anything but the *deliberate* policy of violence pursued by this particular union; and we do not believe for a moment that Mr. Gompers is a fool, whatever else he may be.

Burns said: "I dare Gompers to put his statement that he knew nothing of the dynamite plot into an affidavit. I'm willing to make an affidavit that Gompers went to Indianapolis and sat and talked with men who worked with the McNamaras."

Gompers could do nothing but ignore the challenge.

26

Gompers' Innocence Abroad (1918)[1]

When America entered the First World War, the Wilson administration used Gompers' contacts abroad to sustain the Allied effort. After much haggling and confusion Gompers embarked on a wartime voyage which took him to both the Italian and French battlefronts and brought him into agitated contact with world trade union leaders whose enthusiasm for the war cooled just as Gompers' (and the American) belligerence warmed. Earlier delegations of American labor leaders (without Gompers' presence) impressed British observers as provincial, filled with an "antiquated formality." "They sat like Sphinxes," a British Labour party leader wrote.

The hostility of the A.F.L. to any suggestion of negotiations with the enemy encouraged both the British and American governments to think of ways in which by an exchange of contacts the American labour leaders might stiffen the military ardour of their opposite numbers in Europe. The British Cabinet hoped that Samuel Gompers himself would visit England; but the work entrusted to him by President Wilson to assist the mobilization necessary for the American war effort prevented him from leaving the United States for the time being. Towards the end of 1917, however, Gompers felt it a patriotic duty to do something about the position in England; for Wilson, alarmed by intelligence reports from London about the growing strength of the "peace by negotiation" movement, asked him to suggest some means "by which he could help to steer Mr. Henderson." Gompers therefore invited G. N. Barnes, the new representative of Labour in the British War Cabinet, to select a delegation of British labour leaders to visit America.

One labour delegation had already visited America since the United

[1] From Henry M. Pelling, *America and the British Left* (New York: New York University Press, 1957), pp. 113–14, 122–29. Reprinted by permission of New York University Press and A. & C. Black Ltd.

States had entered the war: but Gompers had not been entirely satisfied with it, although it had given much useful advice on the problems which confronted trade unions in wartime. Gompers had asked
Lloyd George to send on the delegation his old friend W. A. Appleton, the General Secretary of the General Federation of Trade Unions.
Gompers knew, of course, that Appleton was hostile to Socialism, and
had no connection with the Labour Party. . . .

Gompers duly arrived in England, accompanied by a small group
of A.F.L. colleagues, and proceeded first to the annual congress of the
T.U.C. at Derby. While he was there he met Henderson and Mac-
Donald and found them "surprisingly cordial." But it was the support which their policy had at Derby which made the greatest impression upon him. Gompers apparently decided then and there that
it was no use fighting against the alliance of the T.U.C. and the
Labour Party; one could negotiate with this alliance, and secure compromise terms, but one could not destroy it. The correspondent of the
London *Nation* described how this occurred:

> The very gesture with which he swept away a part of his notes, and
> announced that he was "shortening his line on the international front,"
> was an eloquent testimony to the impression which the Congress had
> already made upon him.

Later in the month Gompers and his group attended the Inter-Allied
Labour and Socialist Conference in London which Henderson had
arranged for them. Their very appearance at a conference which included Socialist representation was, of course, a concession on Gompers's part. But the conference had not begun before an embarrassing
incident took place. The credential cards for the delegates were printed
with the title "Inter-Allied Socialist Conference," instead of "Inter-
Allied Labour and Socialist Conference." Gompers and his associates
refused to sign their cards and were at first not admitted to the hall.

Once they were in their places it seemed that they were doing their
best to dominate the proceedings. Bruce Glasier, an I.L.P. representative, described the scene in the *Labour Leader*:

> Mr. Gompers was well planted in the centre of the hall. The chair-
> man and the delegates could not escape from him. He smoked one
> cigar after another without ceasing even while speaking. He kept his
> hat on most of the time, and seldom troubled to take it off while ad-
> dressing the Conference. He was master of the situation. Not a reso-
> lution or amendment could be adopted without his endorsement, and
> none which did not (if a pretext could be found) express acknowledg-
> ment to President Wilson and the American Federation of Labour.

Mrs. Webb's account of the conference in her diary reveals a similar irritation with the visitors: according to her, they

> . . . altogether outshone the I.L.P. in sanctimonious self-righteousness, and high-sounding declaration of ultra-democratic principles. They asserted and re-asserted that the war—at any rate since they entered it—has been a war between Democracy and Disinterestedness, on the one hand, and Autocracy and Lust of Power on the other. Whenever this thesis was controverted the Americans repeated their credo—more slowly, more loudly, and alas at greater length. "Are you stupid, criminal, or merely deaf?" was implied in their intonation, whenever the I.L.P. delegates expressed their pacifist sentiments.

The American conference technique, however much to the distaste of the British representatives, was not employed without effect. Gompers induced the conference to hold its meeting in public and not in private, and thereby obliged Henderson, J. H. Thomas and other British labour leaders to adopt a more vigorous pro-war tone than they would otherwise have done. According to Buckler,

> Had Henderson and Thomas not assumed a distinctly anti-pacifist attitude, they would have placed themselves in the foolish position of openly antagonizing Mr. Gompers, the ardent supporter of President Wilson whom Henderson and Thomas are constantly extolling.

W. Stephen Sanders, the pro-war British Socialist who was attached to the Gompers mission as a British Government agent, took the same view. Gompers's attitude, he said,

> . . . undoubtedly helped to rally the anti-pacifist sections of the conference, who were much more vigorous than usual in the debates that took place.

Gompers also received a letter of congratulation from the veteran Socialist H. M. Hyndman upon his "admirable stand." Nevertheless, the Americans won no support at the conference, except from the Canadians and from an Italian labour group, for their attempt to defeat the plans to arrange a meeting with enemy Socialists.

On the whole, both Gompers and Henderson were satisfied with the outcome of the conference. Both of them were realists, and both knew that it was essential for the British and American labour movements to come to some sort of understanding. Henderson had undertaken to ignore the American Socialists, and to accept the A.F.L. as the sole organ of American labour; Gompers had in turn recognized that Appleton's General Federation of Trade Unions did not represent British labour. Gompers had attended an Inter-Allied Conference which included Socialist representation; but he had maintained his refusal to negotiate with the enemy, and he had stiffened the declarations of the conference on the prosecution of the war. Henderson had secured an agreed statement of war aims on Wilsonian lines, and was still free to act on the majority decision in favour of discussions with the enemy Socialists. As before, the group which was most disgruntled by the performance of the American delegates was the I.L.P.: Mrs. Snowden said that the only satisfactory result of the conference was that "they had taught the representatives of American labour that they did not own the earth"; and MacDonald said that the A.F.L. delegates were "four years out of date, and on labour politics they were half a century out of date."

By this time, however, the German resistance to the growing Allied armies in France was weakening, and overtures for peace were made within a few weeks of the Inter-Allied Conference. Although Gompers's deputy at Washington, John R. Alpine, sent Wilson a telegram in October urging him to ignore these approaches and to "batter away at enemy lines until the road is cleared to Berlin," the overtures quickly led to an armistice on November 11th and the war was over.

The brief period of wartime relations between the British and American labour movements, which has now been described, illustrates some of the difficult problems which beset Anglo-American understanding in this field. In the course of these eighteen months it became clear that while British Liberals and Labour leaders alike expressed unbounded enthusiasm for Wilson's war aims, they were profoundly disappointed with the attitude of Gompers and the A.F.L. It is important to recognize that this was not just a matter of personality. The unfavourable impact of Gompers in Britain was due to major differences in the social and political structure of the two countries. Norman Angell, who was in America at various times during the war, wrote to the London monthly *War and Peace* in April 1918 to explain some of these differences, which he realized were likely to cause trouble. Although he was optimistic about the future of American Socialism after the war, he maintained that in 1918 it was largely a creed of foreign immigrants, and pointed out that it had little contact with "organized labour" in the United States, which itself was "confined almost exclusively to the skilled trades." Angell shrewdly observed:

> I do not think that the real difficulties are in matters of international policy—though Mr. Gompers has based his objection upon meeting Germans during the war. The difficulties come from a wider difference of outlook and social policy.

In fact, Gompers's objection to a conference including enemy representatives was based quite as much on the fact that it was to be a Socialist conference as on the fact that it would include representatives of enemy countries. MacDonald was aware of this aspect of the problem:

> The differences between us here and the American Federation do not originate in war policy, but come from fundamental diversities of attitude that have been intensified by different war experiences up to date.

The fact was that Gompers in his war policy was carrying on his long struggle with Socialism—a struggle in which he had been engaged for a quarter of a century inside the American labour movement. The attitude of the British Labour Party, and the control which the Socialists had won over it, seemed to threaten Gompers once again with an enemy that he thought he had vanquished. This confusion of domestic and international issues affected his whole policy, and led him to make such undiplomatic statements as one at a New York reception for the British labour delegation in March, 1918:

> Neither Sidney Webb nor another Sidney Webb in America, could write the platform for the American labor movement. . . .

27

Lucy Robins Lang: Gompers' Golem[1]

Lucy Robins Lang, a disciple of the anarchist Emma Goldman, met Gompers during the early stages of the Tom Mooney appeal—Mooney had been falsely convicted of bomb-throwing during a San Francisco Preparedness march in 1916. Her autobiography provides a rare, personal view of Gompers during his last years.

Outside Gompers's office, in a room in which several men were cooling their heels, I was met by an apparition that only Poe could have imagined—a bony woman with chalk-white, translucent skin on face and hands. Her thin lips were drawn tight as a pale cord, and her eyes were sunk in her skull. She wore loose black garments and ungainly high-laced shoes. This was R. Lee Guard, Miss Guard, Gompers's secretary.

With absolute impersonality she listened to my business, and then informed me that Mr. Gompers could not see me. "There's a war on; you'll have to wait."

"I'd wait if Mooney could wait."

"He'll have to wait, too."

"He'd like to, but Mr. Gompers will have to persuade the hangman."

She looked up then, but she would give me no assurances. I could come back in a day or two. I came back, and again she shook her head. "Will I have to wait till the war is over?"

"Try tomorrow. . . ."

Fitzi wrote that she was having trouble in New York: unions were refusing to be represented at the rally unless it was approved by Gompers. I was stymied in Washington. Stalking into the federation building on my third try, I encountered John Fitzpatrick of Chicago, who had been warming the mourners' bench for two days without getting in to see his boss. "You might as well forget about Sam and do the best you can without him," he said.

[1] From Lucy Robins Lang, *Tomorrow Is Beautiful* (New York: The Macmillan Company, 1948), pp. 125–28, 177–78, 208–10. Reprinted by permission of *Naomi I. Lang*.

But I have never been willing to give up a fight without at least a parting shot at the enemy. I went into a telegraph office and wrote a message to Gompers in pure vitriol. Whatever I had heard Socialists, Anarchists, and Wobblies say about him in the past two decades, whatever union leaders had said in talking about the McNamara case, I put into my letter. "I now understand why," I wrote, "the great masses of workers despise you, curse you, and eagerly await your death." I instructed a messenger to deliver the letter to Gompers in person and to bring back his signature.

A while later, feeling much better, I stopped in to say good-by to the local boys before catching the train to New York. A chorus greeted me: "By God, you've done it! Sam Gompers himself was in here looking for you. He wanted us to send a posse after you. He wants you to call him right away."

When Miss Guard saw me this time, the blood rushed to her parchment cheeks. As she opened the door of the private office, I glanced with embarrassment and satisfaction at the waiting men, and out of the corner of my eye I caught John Fitzpatrick's grin.

The head man of American labor—a stubby, rotund figure—rose and peered at me over his spectacles. His desk was crowded with papers, inkwells of various sizes, penholders of different periods, blotters, stubs of chalk, seals, clippings, and photographs—topped by a monumental clock. I saw my note in the Western Union envelope lying there, and woke up to the realization of what I had done. I felt myself flushing as red as Miss Guard. Gompers's eyes bored into mine with the assurance of a man who is used to having the other person's drop first, but there was a twinkle down deep in them. "So everyone loathes me," he chuckled. "All people despise me and await my death. Are you among them?"

I had nothing to say. I ducked my face into my bag and hunted for my credentials. He waved them away. "Suppose I should die," he said, "what would you do? If you have any good ideas, I might be willing to cooperate."

Two girls who had been filing letters started to giggle. In a moment of great relief, the four of us began to laugh without restraint. I felt at home as all the cordiality of the La Follettes had not been able to make me feel at home. There was no mystery of background between Gompers and me.

"May I speak now?" I asked.

"Anything you have on your mind."

I talked about west coast labor, about Eric Morton, about Schmidty and Caplan, about the whole struggle that had led up to the Mooney case. He closed his eyes and leaned back in his chair immobile. I asked him why he had done nothing to help Mooney, he who could have done so much. "We hate you," I said, "but we know you have power."

He let me pour my heart out. Then, opening his eyes, he ordered one of the secretaries to bring me the folder on the Mooney case— "all of it."

When I finished reading the documents in a corner of his office, I was crushed, as if I had been flung out of his seventh-story window. Our raucous protest rallies, it now appeared to me, had been as futile as a child's tantrum. The victories we thought we had won had actually been achieved by the masterly hand that had pulled wires behind the scene. It was Gompers far more than anyone else who had persuaded the President to appoint a special commission, and he had suggested the members. Gompers's hand had plucked at the governor of California, at the attorney general, at the governors of neighboring states, with the insistent idea of reopening the case. Most astounding of all, it was Gompers who had stirred up the movement to impeach Fickert.

I handed the folder to him, too ashamed for speech. Gently he took my hand. "You are a true daughter of our people," he said.

His kindness helped me to regain my balance. "But why," I asked, "haven't we known all this?"

He peered over his spectacles—a habit of his—and smiled. "Sit down," he said, "and let me try to tell you." He talked about the labor movement, speaking not as a high official but as one who had been a factory worker. He talked of violence in the labor struggle, the violence that the employers used against the labor movement and the counterviolence of the workers, and of the difficult role that the A. F. of L. had to play in protecting its members. He referred to the Molly Maguire movement among the Pennsylvania miners in the seventies and then to the McNamara case. "It taught us a terrible lesson," he said grimly. Since that affair, he had felt that he must operate, as far as possible, without publicity. "We must help our people," he said, "but we must not endanger the labor movement."

I suggested in a very small voice that all our agitation had been futile. "No," he said quickly, "no! I could not have accomplished too much if I had not been able to say that public opinion was on Mooney's side. Besides, we need indignation like yours. It shows a healthy national conscience." He stopped his pacing. "Where do your ideas come from?" he asked abruptly.

"More or less from Emma Goldman," I answered frankly.

"Oh, that's it," he said. He began to talk about the philosophical Anarchists he had known in his early days in the cigar factories. "Some of the gentlest, most spiritual men I have ever encountered," he called them. He talked about his friend Victor Drury, a musician of great ability, who came to this country after the Paris Commune and who deliberatey crushed his hand in a door so that his passion for music would not distract him from his service to the labor movement. He spoke also of his Swedish mentor, Karl Malcolm Ferdinand Laurrell, cigar maker and seafarer, who had given his life to labor and revolutionary movements in Germany and Scandinavia. When I said that I, too, had been a cigar maker, it was as if we had discovered a common ancestor. I said something about the Haymarket martyrs, and he recited almost verbatim the speech he had made to the governor of Illinois. "And we accomplished nothing," he said.

"Will that be repeated in the Mooney case?" I asked.

Gompers struck the desk with his fist, and in his bearing was a proud awareness of thirty years of labor progress. "It will not be repeated!" he said. . . .

Agursky[2] wanted to meet Gompers, and finally, after some hesitation, the interview was arranged. "Let us understand each other from the beginning," the Old Man said, pointing to a copy of Lenin's famous pamphlet, "An Open Letter to American Workers." "Tell Mr. Lenin that our 'rope of sand' will prove stronger than his iron chains."

Agursky launched into a vigorous and even eloquent defense of Lenin's suppression of civil liberties. Gompers interrupted him: "Have we been fighting czarism all these years just for a change of chains?"

"This is the only way to establish a Socialist state," Agursky said.

"You may be right, young man," Gompers replied. "But then a Socialist state is simply a slave state."

Persistently Gompers interrogated the Soviet emissary, asking him questions about every aspect of life in Russia. He picked up Lenin's pamphlet again. "This is the man who is going to advise American workers," he said, "and he lumps me and Morris Hillquit together. He does not know that all our lives we have been political opponents."

"He says that you are both reactionaries," Agursky answered, "and so you are."

"Lenin is the greatest reactionary alive today. What does he tell the American Communists?" He opened the pamphlet. "He tells them to practice trickery, to employ cunning, to resort to illegal methods in order to penetrate the trade-unions. He would gladly destroy every gain that American labor had made. He wants us to go back to slavery."

As he was leaving, Agursky said, "Mr. Gompers, I asked to meet you, but I was nevertheless afraid that you would turn me over to the police. I am afraid you would not fare so well in Soviet Russia."

"Young man," Gompers shouted, pointing his finger at him, "call

[2] [Commissar Agursky was sent by the Bolshevik government to coordinate labor radicalism in America during the 1920s.]

on me if the police bother you. I will do anything I can for you—anything but let myself be liquidated." All of us burst into laughter. . . .

There is a Jewish legend that anticipates the story of Frankenstein and his monster. In the latter part of the sixteenth century, when the Jews of Prague were in constant fear of attack, their saintly leader, Rabbi Löw, an ancestor of Justice Brandeis, created a golem, a figure of clay, and, through his mystical powers, endowed it with life. It was the rabbi's intention that this creature should protect the persecuted Jews, but the golem, acquiring human passions, turned upon its master and tried to destroy him. This theme has inspired many writers, and a play called *The Golem* had a considerable success in the late 1920's. During a performance of the play. William Green, who had succeeded Gompers as president of the A. F. of L., whispered to me, "Now I can understand the last years of Sam's life."

Gompers felt that the years that remained to him after he reached the age of seventy were a kind of heavenly dividend, and he sought to use them in ordering the affairs of the great labor body he had created. He had always believed in individual initiative and self-government, and his belief was strengthened by the rise of totalitarianism in parts of Europe; but he could not fail to see that these principles gave scope to forces that endangered the labor movement. Poor and ignorant workers naturally supported the leader who improved their lot, without inquiring too closely into the methods he employed. In labor as in politics, democracy permitted the demagogue to flourish and to wax fat on graft. The labor racketeer was one of Gompers's golems.

The problem was how to eliminate corruption without destroying the democracy of the unions. Convinced that the unions must cure their own evils, Gompers fought against any suggestion of government interference. Thus he sometimes found himself in the position of resisting public attacks on labor officials whom he was fighting with all his might within the movement.

Such was the situation that arose in the case of Robert Brindell, a burly, boisterous, unscrupulous leader of the New York City building trades. His conduct created such a scandal that the state legislature set up an investigating committee, with Charles C. Lockwood as chairman and Samuel Untermeyer as counsel. Untermeyer invited Gompers to testify. Gompers agreed to do so, but only on the understanding that he could refrain from answering questions if he saw fit. He asked me to act as his representative in an informal talk with Untermeyer. "Tell Sam he needn't be afraid of me," the lawyer said. "I'm the one who ought to be scared."

A large audience gathered to watch the duel between the two Sams. For two days the aged president of the A. F. of L. appeared on the witness stand, often feigning timidity to lead the famous attorney on, and then delivering a bold stroke that paralyzed him. Steadfastly he opposed any governmental interference in such matters as jurisdictional conflicts, restriction of membership, misappropriation of union funds, and conflicts between unions and employers. That evils existed he did not deny, but he argued that they would only be aggravated by the passing of laws.

"You have no faith in the courts?" Untermeyer asked him.

"Very little."

"Would you permit any kind of review in the courts concerning the expulsion of a member of a labor union?"

"I would not."

"You would allow that injustice to remain unredressed until the enlightenment of the labor movement has reached the state at which expulsion would no longer exist?"

"I would, yes."

"You believe that the courts are closed to the poor, don't you?"

"Very nearly so."

One of Gompers's tricks caused the audience a good deal of amusement. Whenever Untermeyer had him cornered, he would dramatically motion to Oyster to come to him, and then, excusing himself to Untermeyer and the committee, he would stride slowly down the aisle on his well dressed secretary's arm and enter the men's room. This performance was repeated again and again, and the more the audience laughed, the more indignant Untermeyer grew. At the noon recess, as we walked through the chamber, with Gompers leaning on me, Untermeyer placed his arm around the shoulders of the stubby labor leader. "Now, look here, Sam. You've got to quit this nonsense of running to the toilet every time I have the upper hand. You know very well that I can stop you if I have to."

Gompers looked up at him. "Can you? Why not try it, then, and take the consequences?"

PART THREE

GOMPERS IN HISTORY

"Wisdom and understanding do not always accompany diplomas, degrees, or attach themselves to endowed chairs."

—SAMUEL GOMPERS (1913)

Samuel Gompers' historical reputation is not very good. Labor history specialists, with few exceptions, have accepted the conclusions of the first major chroniclers of the AFL, John R. Commons, his students, and collaborators. These judgments of the man are tied to critiques of the organization he built and its role during the emergence of industrial America.

Historians who are not labor specialists write of Gompers as if he were an animated icon, a symbol for ritualistic beliefs and practices. (One scholar calls him the "great Totem" of American labor.)

In our time part of the difficulty in making historical judgments about Gompers concerns the enduring force of issues he confronted then and which remain with us even now: e.g., the role of organized labor in society, questions of war and peace, color discrimination, craft exclusivity, and union corruption. The political and ideological attitudes of historians naturally affect the history they write. Therefore, Gompers' reputation, past and present, has a peculiar unity. Hopefully, the following writers will provide notes for conclusions, not definitive judgments.

28

John R. Commons: Karl Marx and Samuel Gompers[1]

Professor John R. Commons knew Gompers and worked with him for over twenty years on labor problems. This essay is both a review of Gompers' autobiography and a generous eulogy. Commons (and in later years his students and associates) upheld Gompers' pragmatism, his "pure and simple" philosophy, and his shrewd faith in organized power.

It is interesting to compare the theories of the two great Jewish leaders of labor movements, Karl Marx and Samuel Gompers. Gompers' *Autobiography* stands for American trade unionism where Marx's *Communist Manifesto* and *Das Kapital* stand for international Socialism. Each is an economic interpretation of history and each is a program of action based on that interpretation.

Marx got his education in the German universities and did his investigating in the British Museum. Gompers left the public schools of London at the age of ten and got his education in Cooper Union, but did his investigating in the cigar shops of New York. Marx converted the dominant philosophy of his time from Hegel's idealism of a future German Empire into the economic materialism of a future world Communism. Gompers learned the *Communist Manifesto* and Marx's theories from the socialist exiles from Europe, and it was "this insight into a world of hidden thought," he says, "that aroused me to master the German language in order that I might read for myself." What he learned from Marx was this: "Economic organization and control over economic power were the fulcrum which made possible influence and power over other fields. Control over the basic things of life gives power that may be used for good in every relationship of life." This, he says, was the "fundamental concept on which the A. F. of L. was later developed."

Gompers recites that Marx was primarily a trade unionist, and that

[1] From John R. Commons, "Karl Marx and Samuel Gompers," *Political Science Quarterly*, 41 (June 1926): 281–86. Reprinted by permission of The Academy of Political Science.

he opposed both the political and anarchistic elements in the labor movement. But it was, as he says, "the Lassallean program of political action that won over the militant economic program of Marx both in Germany and France," and it was the Anarchists, led by Bakunin, who succeeded in splitting, in 1872, the International Workingmen's Association, which Marx and the British trade unions had formed in 1864. This split and the reaction in Europe drove to America, in the early seventies, the Marxian Socialists, but apparently without the Lassallean Socialists or Anarchists. The latter did not come in numbers until after the German anti-Socialist law of 1878, although there was a "large sprinkling" of French Communists in New York after the downfall of the Paris Commune.

Gompers's intimate associates were the Marxian Socialists, from about 1873 to 1878. There was F. A. Sorge, Marx's friend and successor as executive of the International Workingmen's Association when the headquarters were moved from London to New York to escape the Anarchists, where Sorge "was in charge of the disintegration that followed." There was J. P. McDonnell who "had spent several years in London in the office of Karl Marx." There was David Kronburg, "easily the master mind," a member of the International. There was P. J. McGuire, a member of the I. W. A., "a fiery young orator with a big heart, and as yet immature judgment." Especially was there Ferdinand Laurrell, to whose memory Gompers dedicated this autobiography as "a workman all his life who was my mental guide through many of my early struggles." Laurrell "had been in the inner circles of Marx's International and knew more of its connections with European revolutions than was generally known." He was a Swede and had been secretary of the International for the three Scandinavian countries, and "knew from experience the revolutionists, the socialists, the anarchists, and the trade unionists. . . . Strong and vigorous mentally and physically, he forged to the head of both the revolutionary and labor movements."

Gompers makes it quite plain that Laurrell was his teacher, who carried him through an investigation of all the philosophies and tactics of all schools of the various labor movements, besides critically examining Gompers's own theories.

> I remember going to him one day and enthusiastically telling him some wild plans I had for human betterment. When I had finished, convinced that I had talked well, I sat back with manifest satisfaction to let Laurrell reply. He had been working silently, but had not missed a point, and I began to feel physically smaller as Laurrell systematically and ruthlessly demolished my every statement. By the time he had finished

> I vowed to myself "Never again will I talk that stuff—but I will find principles that will stand the test."

Again, "in those days I was full of fire and dreams and burning with sentiment, and I might have followed any course or associated myself with any movement that seemed to promise freedom for my pals and fellow workers. It was the wise counsel of my friend Laurrell that saved me: 'Never permit sentiment to lead you, but let intellect dominate action.' " Also Laurrell advised him to attend the Socialist meetings, "listen to what they have to say and understand them, but do not join the Party." Gompers never joined, but it was his habit to attend their Saturday evening meetings.

Indeed, Ferdinand Laurrell conducted a remarkable research seminar in economics in the only union cigar shop in New York, owned by David Hirsch, one of the German exiles, and an employer of fifty or sixty exiles and others. Gompers entered this shop in 1873, at the age of twenty-three, having been working at his trade in New York since 1863, and he remained there five years, and afterwards worked in other shops until 1887, altogether twenty-four years in a cigar shop.

In Hirsch's shop the workers subscribed to labor and other papers, read aloud to each other while they worked and conducted a "labor forum." Piece work, hand work, skilled work, quiet work, no rules against talking, and Ferdinand Laurrell made Gompers an "intellectual."

Gompers joined also, during the seventies, a group of labor investigators, *die zehn Philosphen*," who were, in fact, "an inner circle" of the International Workingmen's Association. At least three of these philosophers, including Gompers, afterwards became well known leaders in the American Federation of Labor.

> We dreamed together and then thrashed out our dreams to see what might be of practical value. From this little group came the purpose and initiative that finally resulted in the present American labor movement—the most effective economic organization in the world. We did not create the American trade union—that is the product of forces and conditions. But we did create the technique that guided trade unions to constructive policies and achievements.

Then, in 1877, came "the great strike" of New York cigar makers against the tenement-house system. The strike was partly compromised but mainly lost. Gompers's job at Hirsch's was filled. He had pawned everything but his wife's wedding ring. Eventually he found another job, but he moved to cheaper quarters in a distant part of Brooklyn, so that, on account of the distance and the needs of his family, he imagined himself separated from active work in the labor movement. But his union made him chairman of a committee on administration. He moved back to New York. "That, in my opinion, was the turning point of my life."

Following this disastrous strike, Gompers and his associates began to reorganize the cigarmakers, basing their plans on the experience of their own weakness, on the trade-union philosophy of the ten philosophers, and on a Marxism revised to fit American conditions.

I mention these five years of Gompers's life because occasionally scholastic critics speak of him as having no theories, no philosophies, no understanding of the "intellectuals," no science, no ultimate goal, but as merely a man of cunning, pugnacity, intuition, expediency and honesty. Yet, as I see such things, he was the greatest "intellectual" of them all and the most scientific of the theorists. Here was a true experimenter in the science of economics, trying out his theories on one of the most experienced teachers of the subject and on the ten philosophers, in what would now be called a set of research seminars, and all the while trying them out on the world of industry where he worked. Here was a continual revision of theories until one was found that would work—and the American Federation of Labor was the way it worked. This, I suspect, is the truly scientific method, and those who pride themselves on being the intellectuals, whom Gompers learned to reject, would scarcely nowadays, in sciences other than economics, be permitted to have respectful, much less patient, attention. Gompers says of himself, "at no time in my life have I worked out definitely articulated economic theory," but have reached conclusions gradually, "after discarding proposals to which I temporarily subscribed." Which is the *greater* intellect, I do not know—the brilliant scholar who propounds anything or everything and leads nowhere, or the slow-minded Gompers or Darwin who works patiently for decades, theorizing and experimenting? Which is the more *scientific* intellect there seems to be no doubt.

The Marxian philosophy has, it is true, been described by its followers as "scientific" Socialism. What Marx did was to take Ricardo's economics and Hegel's philosophy, and to find in the one the secret of "control over the basic things of life" and in the other the clue that would trace that control through all history from primitive communism to world-communism. He did, as Gompers did not, build an "articulated economic theory" and provided not only a string to carry his mass of facts, but also a visibly articulated goal where the string ended. Gompers's experimental method had neither a fixed mechanism for reaching the goal nor even a visible goal. While Marx's mechanism and goal were government, Gompers's mechanism and goal were liberty. With Marx the individual was subordinate, in every respect and at all times, to a government of some kind that controls the economic foundations. With Gompers the individual was supreme but coerced, and was to acquire liberty by collectively imposing shop rules for control of the economic foundations. This difference appears in their theories regarding trade unions.

Gompers maintains that "whatever modifications Marx may have taught in his philosophical writings, as a practical policy he urged the formation of trade unions and the use of them to deal with the problems of the labor movement." He cites Marx's letters, and, of course, he knew this fact from Marx's intimate followers. Marx was, indeed, closely affiliated with the British trade-union leaders in the decade of the sixties, during a part of his long residence in London. But the trade unions of the sixties and seventies, as Gompers frequently makes note, had no very clear distinctions in philosophy or tactics that might keep them separate from those who were not wage-earners, and hence they had no rules that held the unions to the actual economic problems of the shop as against the general reforms of anarchism, socialism, politics, in which non-wage-earners were adepts. Here it was Laurrell, again, who gave him the cue, fashioned on his own wide experience: " 'Study your union card, Sam, and if the idea doesn't square with that, it ain't true.' My trade union card came to be my standard in all new problems."

In this way, eventually, Gompers became even more class-conscious than Marx himself, for Marx's International Workingmen's Association admitted all classes of labor reformers to membership and it was this that eventually caused the British unions to withdraw and the Association itself to split on the rocks of Anarchism and Socialism. But the significant thing was not merely that the "intellectuals" were admitted to the labor unions, but that the unions were thereby diverted from attention to the shop rules, which, in American and British unions since that time, have been imposed in such abundance for the protection of the individual worker on the job. The intellectuals looked upon labor as a mass, and it was the "solidarity" of labor to which Marx looked for the conquest of capitalism *en masse*. The individual worker did not count for much. But for Gompers and his teacher, Laurrell, who were workers themselves, it was the individuality of the laborer that counted, and economic power for them meant power of the union to protect the individual in his job. Previously it had been wages and hours for all as a class—now it became, also, how to prevent the employer from using his economic power arbitrarily against the individual. Henceforward "recognition of the union," "grievance committees," "business agents," union cards, arbitration, hiring, firing, restrictions on speeding up, promotions, transfers, even such small items as priority in having the better place to work in the shop—these became the economic foundations of individual liberty for the wage-earners, and for Gompers as one of them.

Needless to say, these small matters could not attract the attention of Karl Marx or the intellectuals or the revolutionaries—they were interested in large things such as the world production of wealth, but these shop rules restricted output. They were interested in who should get the whole product of the whole social-labor-power, but these rules turned on the petty sorrows, oppressions and envies of individuals hidden away under the mass. Somewhere even Marx decries these restrictive policies of trade unions which stood in the way of raising labor as a class, and the German trade unions did not resort to them until after the Great War. They had previously relied on politics and ultimate socialism, rather than on what Gompers would call self-help in the shop. Yet these shop rules are all-important for the individual worker, for they are his liberty.

Finally, when Gompers and the others built up the American Federation of Labor, they did not have a centralized big union where Gompers would be a dictator and have control of the funds and discipline, but a loose federation, with shop autonomy, union autonomy, craft autonomy—"autonomy" everywhere, and only two rules—union card and no dual unions. There was no ultimate goal about such an arrangement, and little that could satisfy an intellectual who idealizes order and logic, but it was liberty through control of economic power.

There is scarcely space to summarize further how Gompers "learned the weakness of radical tactics," the weaknesses of legislation, the injury done to labor organization by "intellectuals," his account of the "fight to the finish" with the Knights of Labor who included intellectuals and represented the idea of centralized labor government, his account of "socialists as I know them," of the injunction, and of the part he played in the Great War. All of these have as their central theme, "Liberty through Economic Power."

29

Philip S. Foner:
Class Collaborator[1]

What Commons considered pragmatic maneuvering on behalf of the workers, more stringent Marxists regarded as mere "class collaboration." Professor Philip S. Foner, a leading student of American labor, uses the stencil of Marxism–Leninism to trace the "failure" of Gompers to lead American workers out from materialism and into class revolution. The following essay tries to explain the paradox of Gompers' early radicalism and his later moderation.

Gompers once proudly reported: "At no time in my life have I worked out definitely an articulated economic theory." Yet in the late 'eighties and early 'nineties, he did "work out" the tactics and strategy of the youthful A. F. of L., many of which continued to influence the Federation for years to come.

Despite his awareness that there was a long and varied history of the American labor movement from colonial times to the last quarter of the nineteenth century, Gompers believed that trade unionism in the United States at the time the A. F. of L. was founded was "practically in its infancy." By this he meant that the bargaining power of the workers was still puny in a period when the tendency was towards greater and greater "concentration of wealth and power" in industry. Compared with the "lightning rapidity" with which power was concentrating in the hands of the capitalist class, the labor movement had been moving "with the gait of a stage coach."

To bring the labor movement to a level where it could cope with the growing power of capital, it was essential, Gompers argued, that the A. F. of L. should avoid the errors of the past that had largely been responsible for preventing organized labor from emerging from its

[1] From Philip S. Foner, *History of the Labor Movement in the United States*, vol. 2, *From the Founding of the American Federation of Labor to the Emergence of American Imperialism* (New York: International Publishers Co., Inc., 1955), pp. 174–77, 185–88, 439. Reprinted by permission of the publisher.

infancy. "We do not wish to raise a structure," he wrote in June, 1887, "whose foundations are rotten, being built up by repeating the errors of others who have preceded us."

What were the errors of the past that Gompers sought to avoid in building the Federation on a foundation which would make it possible both to survive and to forge ahead?

One was the practice, seen clearly in the case of the K. or L., of permitting all sorts of non-working class elements, including even employers, to belong to a labor union. Specifically criticizing the K. of L.'s policy of permitting employers to become members, Gompers pointed out that this "very frequently deterred working men from seeking an improvement in their condition by reason of fear in giving offence to such employers."

In dozens of letters, Gompers emphasized that "the members of Unions affiliated with the American Federation of Labor must be exclusively wage-earners. None other can be admitted." There was room for nen-working class elements, even employers, to work jointly with the trade unions in broad, progressive movements, but the unions must be reserved for the worker, whom Gompers defined as "one who receives wages for his work as in contradistinction to the wage payer." He had learned from "the honored dead Karl Marx," whose works he had read in German,[2] the all-important significance of this principle in labor struggles. In a letter, dated October 8, 1890, Gompers, paraphrasing Marx, stated the case succinctly: "The A. F. of L. holds it as a self-evident maxim that the emancipation of the working class must be achieved by the working classes themselves. There is no doubt that men with the best intentions outside of the ranks of labor can aid in the movement. We court their co-operation, their sympathy and their advice but cannot give into their hands the direction of the affairs which rightfully belong to and must be exercised by the wage workers."

Another danger arising from allowing non-working class elements to enter the trade unions was that they tended to divert the workers' organizations from the immediate problems facing them. A major error of the past which flowed from this, in Gompers' judgment, was hitching the labor movement to the wagons of different panacea-peddlers who promised an easy solution to all of the problems of the working class. In this category he placed such utopian nostrums as the single tax, currency reform, producers' cooperatives, and other enticing all-

---

[2] In his autobiography, *Seventy Years of Life and Labor,* Gompers asserts that he studied German with special diligence so that he might read Marx. In an interview with a reporter for the Detroit *Free Press* in 1896, he emphasized the same point, and added in his own handwriting to the printed report of the interview that he did this "to be of greater service to the [labor] movement." (Detroit *Free Press,* Oct. 18, 1896.)

embracing plans to lift the working class out of wage slavery by a short-cut route. "The ills of our social and economic system," Gompers wrote, "cannot be cured by patent medicine."

One of Gompers' chief objections to the middle class reformist panaceas was that they tended to push the class truggle out of the minds of the workers by spreading illusions that they could be transformed into farmers, independent business men or cooperative self-employers in an economic system under which workers were likely to remain workers throughout their lives. "When the laboring man becomes an investor even in a small way he is less liable to engage in a conflict between labor and capital," Gompers wrote in 1892. Regarding trade unions as only a temporary necessity until he became an entrepreneur, the worker who was influenced by the panacea-peddler would not make the necessary contributions and sacrifices to build stable unions capable of combatting the "avarice of the capitalist classes."

In later years, Gompers denied the existence of the class struggle, but not so in the period when the A. F. of L. was taking form. In the initial number of the *Union Advocate,* June, 1887, Gompers wrote: "Life is at best a hard struggle with contending forces. The life of the toiler is made doubly so by the avarice of the arrogant and tyrannical employing classes. Greedy and overbearing as they are, trying at nearly all times to get their pound of flesh out of the workers, it is necessary to form organizations of the toilers to prevent these tendencies more strongly developing, as wealth is concentrating itself into fewer hands to prevent engulfing and drowning us in an abyss of hopelessness and despair."

Gompers had only scorn for the doctrines spread by Powderly and other leaders of the Knights which proclaimed that the interests of labor and capital were identical and harmonious. He stated flatly, at this time, that it was impossible to have harmonious relations with "cruel and iniquitous employers and companies who think more of dividends than of human hearts and bodies." "The production of profits," Gompers emphasized, "is the primary and constant object of the capitalistic system." Under this system, the blood of the workers was "being used as the lubricating oil for the machines that grind their very bones into cash to gratify the wishes of the insatiable monsters whose only deity was the almightly dollar." To think of harmonious relations between labor and capital under such a system was the height of folly. "I think that the struggles of labor cannot be obviated in the future," Gompers stated categorically in 1892. He set forth his "credo" for this period in the following statement: "From my earliest understanding of the conditions that prevail in the industrial world, I have been convinced that I have asserted that the economic interests of the employing class and the workers are not harmonious. . . . There are times when for temporary purposes, interests are reconciled, but they are temporary only."

Disagreeing sharply with those leaders of the Knights who regarded strikes as an outmoded "relic of barbarism," Gompers gave unswerving support to labor's right to strike. In an interview in the New York *World* in April, 1890, Gompers declared that the A. F. of L. had found through experience that strikes were often "the only means whereby the rightful demands of labor can be secured." As he saw it, "the strike is the most highly civilized method which the workers, the wealth producers, have yet devised to protest against wrong and injustice. . . ."

The emancipation of the working class from the capitalist system, Gompers announced, was one of the objects of the youthful A. F. of L. Gompers' letters of this period contain frequent references to this theme. "I believe with the most advanced thinkers as to ultimate ends including the abolition of the wage system," he wrote in 1887. He was to repeat this sentence in many of his letters during these early years of the A. F. of L., always being careful, however, to link together the struggle for immediate demands and the ultimate goal of emancipation from wage slavery under the capitalist system. He insisted that only through the day-to-day struggles around "conditions that prevail in the shop, the factory, the mill and the mine; the question of higher wages, less hours of labor, less obnoxious rules and conditions," could the working class be effectively mobilized for the final emancipation from wage slavery. As he put it, once again paraphrasing Marx: "Out of the improvements in these respects are evolved the necessary stamina, manhood, independence and intelligence which prepare the workers for a higher and nobler civilization, but without these elementary improvements disaster is the result."

During these years, Gompers frequently evaluated issues and demands in terms of the relationship between the immediate struggles and the ultimate goal of the working class. Thus he objected to Henry George's single tax theory on the ground that it "does not promise present reform, nor an ultimate solution." He suggested to an organizer about to set out on an educational tour among A. F. of L. unions that the single tax as an issue be omitted from the discussion since it was "not a living material issue upon which the workers depend for amelioration and final emancipation."

In his correspondence with European Socialist and labor leaders, Gompers made it clear that the A. F. of L.'s ultimate aim was the emancipation of the working class from capitalist wage slavery. One of his letters to Victor Delahaye, to be read to a gathering of French workers, opened: "Comrades, Though oceans divide us, the same spirit

and purpose prompts us to seek in organization and the final emancipation of the Proletariat of the World." . . .

Gompers' statements on labor solidarity like those on the class struggle, the emancipation of labor from wage slavery, and others of his
militant and radical utterances which are quoted above will certainly
sound startling to those who know that Gompers spent much of his
time during his long career as A. F. of L. president in combatting
these very principles. The question naturally arises: Was there a
fundamental difference between Gompers of the early Federation and
Gompers after the late 1890's?

Before answering this question it is important to note that at least
in one respect Gompers remained consistent throughout his tenure as
A. F. of L. president. Consistently and bureaucratically he ignored the
constitution of the A. F. of L. as well as the specific instructions of
the conventions whenever he opposed the policies they advocated. In
the majority of instances, as we shall see, he defied the will of the
A. F. of L. membership, as expressed in conventions, when it favored a
radical and militant program. One example during the early years of
the Federation will illustrate this point. When the Federation con-
vened a few days after the Henry George mayoralty campaign of 1886,
it will be recalled, the delegates enthusiastically adopted a resolution
declaring that the time had arrived for the working people to decide
on united action at the ballot box and also resolved to urge a most
generous support to labor's independent political movement. But
Gompers deliberately sabotaged the convention's decision. Instead of
carrying out the mandate of the Federation, he "stood back and
watched" and "did not let the A. F. of L. become entangled in any
partisan activity. . . ." He even belittled the entire movement for
independent political action in a letter to the United Labor Party's
journal, and refused to say a word for its candidates during the 1887
campaigns, declaring that the questions involved did not affect labor's
interests.

The incident is significant in at least two important respects. For
one thing, it reveals that for all of his progressive and militant utterances, Gompers actually lagged behind the A. F. of L. membership
and even the leaders of the craft unions on the crucial issue of independent working class political action. For another, it discloses that
from the very outset of the Federation, Gompers was a bureacratic
leader who had not the slightest hesitation in defying the will of the
membership.

In addition to being fundamentally a labor bureaucrat, Gompers
was also basically an opportunist who knew how to trim his sails to
the particular situation he faced. Writing to an International Socialist

Congress Gompers could sound very radical indeed; addressing a gathering of business leaders he could sound very conservative. Expressing views at a time when the workers were becoming more radical under the impact of the growing power of monopoly and its domination of the government, Gompers could voice radical sentiments. At a time when many of the mass movements of the workers had been defeated and when the leaders of the craft unions were yielding to the monopolies, he could easily repudiate each and every one of his earlier progressive utterances. In short, Gompers was moved at all times by one consideration only: What would advance the interests of Samuel Gompers and further his career as president of the A. F. of L. In the early years, advancing the career of Samuel Gompers meant building the Federation since obviously unless the organization he headed attracted workers his position as president meant nothing. And from the very outset of the Federation, Gompers adopted the attitude that he had a vested interest in his job as president.

Gompers were shrewd enough to understand that during the early years of the A. F. of L. he was addressing workers who had gone through the militant struggles of the 'eighties and were deeply influenced by Socialist thought and by the principles of labor solidarity emphasized by the K. of L. To attract these workers to the A. F. of L., it was necessary to convince them that the Federation did not reject the class struggle or the ultimate goal of a new social system and that it continued the finest traditions of the Knights while disposing of those features which were hastening the Order's decline. To be sure, Gompers knew how to keep his radical utterances sufficiently vague and general as to render them often meaningless.[3] Nevertheless, he knew enough to advocate radical principles when these would advance his own position in the labor movement, and he was fully prepared to abandon them the moment he felt that they were proving to be an obstacle to his career.

Gompers had risen to leadership in his own organization, the Cigar Makers International Union, by advocating the principles of industrial unionism and by combatting the exclusive admission requirements under which the International not only refused to admit the unskilled and semiskilled workers in the trade, but forbade its members to work in the same shop with them. Realizing that the union was doomed if it did not abandon its restrictive policies and that industrial unionism was growing more and more popular among the cigar makers, Gompers stressed the importance of uniting all the workers, skilled and un-

---

[3] His statements about the "future development" of society and "emancipation of labor" were extremely vague, and he never really specified the nature of the future society. The closest he came to it was to express the view, privately, that the trade unions were "the germ of the future state."

skilled, and permitting all branches of the industry to be eligible for membership, whether they worked by hand, mold, or machine.

Gompers understood that many workers had been deeply influenced by the K. of L.'s emphasis upon industrial unionism as opposed to craft organization of the skilled workers only. Hence he began to champion a form of industrial unionism during these early years. In 1888 he recommended to the Federation that in the near future the basis of the A. F. of L. should be modeled on industrial divisions which would hold their own conventions, legislate on subjects that affected the general interests of their particular trades and industries, and would, in turn, be represented by their proportionate number of delegates in the conventions of the A. F. of L. With each industrial division having a representative on the Executive Council, the Federation would become a federation of industrial federations rather than a federation of trade unions.

Gompers' proposal ran into the solid opposition of the trade union leaders in the Federation, and he quickly realized that he would never advance his career as A. F. of L. president if he advocated the principles of industrial unionism. He swiftly abandoned the plan and became a staunch defender of craft unionism. In short, Gompers was ready to support a progressive program as long as it would advance his career; the moment he saw that this would actually be an obstacle to his career he not only abandoned the program but became the leading opponent of what he previously had championed.

In abandoning so quickly the proposal for industrial federations, Gompers became a stalwart supporter of trade autonomy. This, of course, made a mockery of his lofty, militant statements. However progressive Gompers sounded in proclaiming what he represented were the principles of the Federation, they had absolutely no binding effect upon the affiliated unions which could and did violate these principles with impunity. Most leaders of the trade unions in the A. F. of L. were prepared to endorse Gompers' lofty statements on labor solidarity as long as they were couched in general terms. They agreed verbally with "the broad and liberal sentiments" he expressed, and that, as P. J. McGuire, second in command of the A. F. of L. put it, "the interests of the working classes are everywhere identical, and we should do all in our power to organize all trades and callings in every city, town and hamlet of the country." But they also made it clear that they regarded the interests of the skilled mechanics as paramount, that they would not consider jeopardizing the craft unions of skilled workers by organizing the unskilled in their trades, and that they did not expect the A. F. of L. to repeat the "tragic mistake" of the K. of L. by uniting skilled and unskilled in the same union.

From the outset, therefore, a conflict developed in the youthful A. F.

of L. between the principles of Labor solidarity and that of craft
narrowness, between the principles enunciated in statements affirming
that the Federation sought to organize all workers regardless of skill,
race, creed, color, sex or national origin and those enunciated and
practiced by the leaders of the craft unions which emphasized primarily
the interests of the skilled mechanics, most of whom were male, white,
and native-American. The nature of this conflict is clearly set forth
in the policy of the A. F. of L. during its formative years towards the
organization of women, Negroes, and foreign-born workers. . . .

The essence of this unionism was class-collaboration on behalf of the
bourgeoisie. On the economic front it stressed the necessity for immediate gains for a small strata of the working class, the skilled craftsmen, and struggled to achieve for this "aristocracy of labor," "job
monopoly," better wages and shorter hours, and very little else, and
this, too, at the expense of the mass of the workers who were unorganized. On the political front, it made the organized workers the tail-kite
to the political parties of the capitalist class. On both fronts, it meant
"policies and methods" which prevented any real expression of the
militancy of the working class, which avoided clashes with the trusts
and the government, and which bought a limited security and higher
wages for the skilled workers at the expense of the rest of the working
class. Between the A. F. of L. craft unions and the industrialists a
broad area of implicit agreement was reached after 1900. "The unions,"
one authority points out, "would make no effort to organize the unskilled and Negro workers; the corporations would make certain concessions to the trade unions."

Yet the earlier militant traditions of the American working class
were never completely destroyed by the imperialist monopolists and
their class-collaboration allies in the labor movement. The struggle
against these class-collaboration policies continued. It was, to be sure,
made more difficult by the mistaken tactics of many of the most militant
elements in the labor movement who isolated themselves from the
masses of workers organized in the craft unions. But the important fact
remains that the struggle did continue—the irreconcilable class struggle against the capitalists, for the organization of the entire working
class in this struggle regardless of skill, race, creed, color, sex or national origin, and for the unity of the workers on the economic and
political fronts. The monopolists and their allies in the A. F. of L.
bureaucracy won many battles in this struggle. But in spite of all the
might on their side and in spite of merciless repression of the militant
workers, they were not able to achieve a prolonged victory over the
working class. . . . [T]hey never succeeded in eradicating the irreconcilable class struggle between labor and capital; they never suc-

ceeded permanently in forcing the workers to compromise with the capitalists at the expense of the entire working class, and they never succeeded in forcing the militant vanguard to subordinate itself to the agents of the monopolists in the labor movement.

30

Daniel Bell: The Great Totem[1]

Professor Daniel Bell, a brilliant sociologist, claims that Gompers' life was a quest for respectability: for himself, for unions, and for workers' power, however limited, in a highly industrialized society. This essay is drawn from a larger study explaining the almost total failure of American socialists to organize and influence significant numbers of workers in modern times.

The early leaders of the American Federation of Labor, Adolph Strasser, P. J. McGuire, and Samuel Gompers, had gone through the sectarian schools of socialist dogmatics. The interminable theoretical wranglings which constituted the curriculum had left them with a skepticism of Marxian politics as applied to the American scene, and helped to shape the here-and-now, pure-and-simple trade unionism of the A.F.L. Because the aims of the Federation were limited to the immediate problem of wages and hours, two important consequences followed. One of these was the decisive rejection, after tentative flirting, of the farmers, Greenbackers, small businessmen, and the various "antimonopoly" political campaigns; such alliances, which proved the undoing of the National Labor Union and the Knights of Labor, merely sucked the worker into the vortex of a swiftly political whirlwind, lifted him high, and dumped him unceremoniously when its force was spent. The second consequence was the open acceptance of the concentration of economic power as an inevitable fact of industrial capitalism. Labor could try to hedge in, but not challenge, the power of the rising new class. On the "trust issue," thus, the new trade-union movement broke with the middle-class and agrarian reformers. These two basic assumptions meant that labor would not stand outside capitalist society and challenge it, but would seek a secure place within

[1] From Daniel Bell, "The Background and Development of Marxian Socialism in the United States," in Donald Drew Egbert and Stow Persons, eds., *Socialism and American Life*, no. 4 in Princeton Studies in American Civilization (Princeton: Princeton University Press, 1952), vol. 1, pp. 249–56. Copyright 1952 by Princeton University Press. Reprinted by permission of the publisher.

it, and, when powerful enough, slowly transform it by demanding a share of power.

These attitudes gain vividness only when interpreted through the life history of Sam Gompers, the man who enunciated them and who, with driving force, created the American labor movement in his own stubborn and pragmatic image. Samuel Gompers is the great totem of the American labor movement, and the rules of endogamy and other taboos he set down have become the prescribed rituals of American labor. A forbidding and stubborn father, the "sons" were reared in his image, retaining all the ritual forms but, except for John L. Lewis,[2] little of the vitality.

Born in 1850, the son of Dutch-Jewish parents, Gompers grew up in London working-class quarters, where he absorbed a sense of his own class; and at the age of thirteen came to the United States. When Gompers was twenty-three he went to work in the cigar shop of David Hirsch, a German revolutionary exile whose factory was the center of many burning theoretical controversies. Cigarmaking at that time was as easy and gregarious operation. The men sat around large tables, talking volubly as their fingers swiftly and mechanically shaped the cigars. In the shop Gompers came under the influence of Karl Ferdinand Laurrell, an ardent Marxist who had been active in the First International. Marxism then meant, however, a fierce trade unionism, as against the political biases of the Lassalleans, and Gompers was quickly won to the trade-union viewpoint. But it was the obstinate manner in which the sectarians ignored the bread-and-butter concerns of the union that soured him completely on the political socialists. At that time the cigarmakers' union faced competition from cheap, low-paid "homeworkers" who made the cigars in their tenement homes. Gompers, as the head of the union, sought legislation outlawing the production of cigars in homes. He marked for reprisal those legislators who voted against the measure and called for support of those who worked for the bill. These men were running on old-line party tickets. But the political socialists were dead-set against voting for old-party candidates, even the prolabor ones, charging that such a move might provide temporary gains for the cigarmakers but corrupt the labor movement and destroy political socialism. Even when the first tenement-house bill was enacted, the socialists refused to support for reelection Gompers' man, Edward Grosse, who had been instrumental in pushing through the measure.

But the Marxist influences left indelible traces in Gompers' philosophy. This was particularly true of the crude "economic determinism"

[2] [Long-time president of the United Mine Workers, founder and early head of the CIO.]

which was characteristic of his view of society. In his autobiography, Gompers wrote sententiously, "Economic power is the basis upon which may be developed power in other fields. It is the foundation of organized society . . . economic organization and control over economic power [are] the fulcrum which made possible influence and power in all other fields. . . . This fundamental concept upon which the A. F. of L. was later developed was at that time not formulated in men's minds."

This conviction underlay Gompers' philosophy of "voluntarism," which consisted, essentially, in a fear of the state. Since the state was a reflection of dominant economic power groups, any state intervention could only lead to domination by big business. Gompers, like the old Manchester liberals, wanted a "negative state." At the 1914 convention of the American Federation of Labor, one delegate asked: "Why, if you are opposed to the eight-hour work day for men by law, did you ask for a law regulating and limiting injunctions?" Gompers replied: "In the law to limit and regulate injunctions we propose to clip the power of the courts insofar as labor is concerned, and in an eight-hour law for men it is to give courts still greater power than they now have. Is there no difference?"

It is an old axiom that men develop loyalties to the institutions they build, and tend to see events from those particular vantage points. In Gompers, we have a case study of the socialist who entered the union movement, began to see the American scene from that perspective, and changed his viewpoints as unionism in the course of its development found a respectable place in American society. For the socialists, however, life was still a triumph of dogma over experience.

Within the Socialist Labor Party, the influence of Sorge, acting as Engels' emissary, had been thrown consistently on the side of the trade-union faction. The defeat of the politicos in 1890 raised hopes that peaceful cooperation between the socialists and Gompers might be reached. But they could not agree. The issue was too fundamental. It arose out of the demand of the socialists within the A.F.L. for the revival of a separate central trades charter in New York City, for they charged the Central Labor Union with insidious Tammany Hall connections. Gompers refused, stating that the constitution of the American Federation of Labor permitted only labor unions and forbade political representation. At the 1890 convention Lucien Sanial, the socialist spokesman, argued that the Socialist Labor Party was a "bona fide" labor body, and that in Europe the socialists had organized the first trade unions and kept them free of capitalist interference. Gompers stated his case with impressive logic: if the Socialist Labor Party were admitted, he asked, why not such other parties as single taxers, anarchists, and Greenbackers? Partisan politics, he added, was a source of disruption and would split the Federation. If the Socialist Labor Party were admitted, it would be the wedge to independent political activity through the S.L.P. or a party dominated by it. Such an action would be construed as an endorsement of socialism and split the American Federation of Labor. It would keep many unions, such as the railroad unions and bricklayers, who were considering joining, from affiliating.

During this debate Gompers used a phrase which has since become famous as descriptive of the intention of the A.F.L. "Unions, pure and simple," he said, "are the natural organization of wage workers to secure their present material and practical improvement and to achieve their final emancipation." Gompers denied in the debate that he was unsympathetic to socialism, but, he said, "the working people are in too great need of immediate improvement[s] in their condition to allow them to forego them in the endeavor to devote their entire energies to an end however beautiful to contemplate. . . . The way out of the wage system is through higher wages."

When Gompers was upheld by a vote of 1,574 to 496, Lucien Sanial, the S.L.P. representative, declared war against the "fakirs" and said that the "Socialists would cram Socialism down the throats of the American workingman."

In the next three years the debate raged fiercely. De Leon argued that the rapid growth of industrial concentration would bring with it the corollary of Marx's law, the increasing misery of the working class. The American Federation of Labor was attacked as seeking to make the workers contented. In turn Gompers charged that the Socialist Labor Party cared less for the strike than for a few more votes and for newspaper circulation. The attacks became personal. De Leon wrote in the *People*: "From this fear of ruining individual prospects arises the slander of socialism on the part of such men as McGuire and Gompers . . . and all other advocates of pure and simple trade union fakism who are secretly plotting for personal advancement with either capitalism or capitalistic politicians."

In 1893, the socialists came within a hair of capturing the American Federation of Labor. Led by Thomas J. Morgan, the secretary of the machinists' union, and J. Mahlon Barnes of the cigarmakers, they introduced a series of planks which demanded compulsory education and the nationalization of mines, railroads, and utilities. Plank ten called for "the collective ownership by the people of all means of production and distribution." They asked that these planks be submitted for "favorable consideration" to the A.F.L. affiliates. After a hectic debate, the phrase "favorable consideration" was deleted by 1,253 to 1,182 but the entire resolution of submission was carried overwhelmingly. The convention also voted to endorse free silver and instructed the executive council to bring about an alliance with the farmers' organizations.

During the year, a large number of unions within the American Federation of Labor voted to endorse the socialist program, and local affiliates were active in politics. But political activity proved fruitless. A report in the A.F.L.'s *Federationist* in November 1894 listed 300 members of the A.F.L. who had been candidates for office, but of whom only a half dozen had been elected. Strasser, Gompers, and McGuire came out unequivocally against plank ten of the program. They charged it would prevent the growth of the organization and discourage many unions from joining. At the 1894 convention, plank ten was defeated through a parliamentary maneuver by 1,217 to 913. The socialists took revenge on Gompers by voting for and electing the miner John McBride for president. The year that followed was the only one during the rest of his life that Gompers was out of office in the American Federation of Labor; and in 1895 he was returned to office once more.

Gompers had now grown quite bitter against the socialists. When De Leon launched the dual Socialist Trades and Labor Alliance—and in Gompers' lexicon dual unionism was the worst of all crimes— Gompers, who was himself no mean polemicist, poured out some vitriol of his own. In an editorial in the *Federationist*, he wrote:

"We note . . . that the work of union wrecking is being taken up by a wing of the so-called socialist party of New York, headed by a professor without a professorship, a shyster lawyer without a brief, and a statistician who furnished figures to the republican, democratic and socialist parties. These three mountebanks, aided by a few unthinking but duped workers, recently launched, from a beer saloon a brand new national organization, with the avowed purpose of crushing every trade union in the country."

A few years later, when De Leon's dual unionism had split the Socialist Labor Party and his union movement was failing, Gompers wrote, ". . . this moribund concern, conceived in iniquity and brutal concubinage with labor's double enemy, greed and ignorance, fashioned into an embryonic phthisical dwarf, born in corruption and filth; and now dying, surrounded by the vultures of its progeny ready to pounce on the emaciated carcass of the corpse."

By 1900 Gompers had shed the socialist influence and even most of its rhetoric. He had no ultimate aim for labor nor was he in favor of replacing private enterprise. He wanted ten cents an hour more and a half hour a day less. At first Gompers fought the socialists on differences in tactics and organizational strategy, later he fought them on the grounds of principle.

It was shortly after this that the A.F.L. took the much debated step of entering the National Civic Federation, an organization of employers, labor, and the public whose chief officers were, in seeming anomaly, Mark Hanna, the Republican political boss and McKinley kingmaker, as president, and Samuel Gompers as first vice-president.[3] Gompers' own explanation of the move indicated his new concerns. "It helped to establish the practice," he wrote, "of accepting labor unions as an integral social element and logically of including their representatives in groups to discuss policies." This was now labor's single ambition: to win acceptance as a "legitimate" social group, equal with business and the church as an established institution of American life. For Gompers, the immigrant boy, it was a personal crusade as well. He sought to win recognition for labor in all civic aspects of American life: an entry and a hearing at the White House; an official voice in the government, i.e., the Department of Labor; respectful relations with employers; representation in community agencies; etc. To become respectable—this was Gompers', and labor's, aim.

The socialist opposition to Gompers consistently iterated two themes: one, the charge of class collaboration; second, the failure to organize the unskilled into industrial unions. In 1897 the Western Federation of Miners, under left-wing socialist leadership, withdrew from the American Federation of Labor and helped form the Western Labor Union, later the American Labor Union, which sought to organize the unskilled along industrial lines and endorsed socialism. To the jealous Gompers this was another instance of the treacherous "dual unionism" of the socialists. In 1902, Max S. Hayes, a socialist leader, introduced a resolution at the A.F.L. convention fully endorsing socialism. After heated debate, the resolution was just barely defeated 4,897 to 4,171, with 387 not voting.

In the fluctuations of socialist power within the American Federation of Labor, 1902 was the peak year, after which the socialist strength declined. This is an incongruous fact, for 1902 was the beginning of rising socialist political influence in the United States. The answer to this paradox is that the socialist vote was never drawn primarily from organized labor—a fact that was one of its fundamental weaknesses.

In 1905 the revolutionary elements in the labor movement launched the I.W.W. (Industrial Workers of the World). Gompers' retort was characteristic. "The Socialists have called another convention to smash the American trade union movement. This is the sixth 'concentrated'

[3] Although Gompers at this point mingled freely with the political and business greats, he would refuse dining invitations at the homes of the wealthy. In his autobiography he relates that he would often go to dinner parties at the homes of industrialists and explain to them labor's viewpoints. But he never dined there, waiting until the end of the discussion to leave and eat outside. It is unlikely that such behavior arose out of a fear of being corrupted. More likely, Gompers, self-conscious of his proletarian origins, used this device to shock his audience pleasurably and to reinforce his own arrogance.

effort in this direction in the past decade. . . ." The literal charge was unfair. Although Debs was present at the founding of the I.W.W., the organization was never socialist nor did it have party endorsement— but Gompers no longer made simple distinctions. In the large, how- ever, the charge was true. Socialism was "dual" to the A.F.L. and suf- fered the consequences. For Marx and Engels, the need for close kin- ship between socialism and the working class was integral to their theory. In America, the practice was deficient. In later years a signifi- cant wing of the Socialist Party, led by Morris Hillquit, sought to modify the party's harsh attitude toward the leadership of the A.F.L., but the differences arising from the contradictory conceptions of labor's course were too strong. The needed unity was impossible to achieve. Since this lack of unity is the basis for one of the crucial questions to be asked regarding the failure of socialism in the United States, the problems in connection with it are worth exploring in more systematic detail.

The first problem was the socialist characterization of the policies of the A.F.L. as "class collaborationist." Shaw once remarked that trade unionism is not socialism, but the capitalism of the proletariat. In one sense this is true. But the corollary that the trade-union leader must become the "labor lieutenant" and "lackey" of the capitalist class is not the literal sequitur. The basis of this charge was that the A.F.L. sought to benefit the skilled workers at the expense of the other sec- tions of the working class by refusing to admit industrial unions. While the socialists may have been correct in the abstract, it was Gompers who showed the keener insight into working-class psychology. In a clumsy manner, he sought to indicate his theoretical differences with the socialists in respect to class attitudes. They only had an intellectual and he a living knowledge of the workers, he felt. "I told [the social- ists]," Gompers wrote, "that the *Klassen Bewusztsein* (class conscious- ness) of which they made so much was not either a fundamental or inherent element, for class consciousness was a mental process shared by all who had imagination." The real social cement, he said, "was *Klassengefühl* (class feeling) . . . that primitive force that had its origin in experience only." And these experiences, for the average workingman, were of a *limiting* nature: the desire for better wages, shorter hours, etc. The skilled workers had accepted their role, had a "commodity" of their own, and were in a position to bargain. Most of the unskilled, many of them immigrants, had no thought of staying in an especially low-paying job, and drifted. They constituted a large reservoir which the capitalist could always use to break strikes or de- press wages. Thus it was difficult to build a permanent organization of men with no particular stake in their jobs. In behalf of the skilled worker, the American Federation of Labor forged the trade agreement as the instrument for exacting a higher price for his commodity, i.e., his skill. Control of the job supply became the prime means of giving the wage worker protection. It also meant that the union became involved in the market problems of the industry. "Business unionism," is inevitable in the maintenance of the union as a stable organization. The necessity of "business unionism"—living in and of the market—is one that the early Socialist Party could not adequately understand.

A second issue was monopoly. Every major American movement of social protest in the last two decades of the nineteenth century and the first decade of the twentieth had been organized around the antimonopoly motif. Gompers felt that monopoly as an outcome of economic growth was unavoidable. Nor did he feel that it could be controlled by the state, which itself was subservient to the powerful economic interests. "The great wrongs attributable to the trusts," he wrote, "are their corrupting influence on the politics of the country, but as the state has always been the representative of the wealthy persons, we shall be compelled to endure its evils until the toilers are organized and educated to the degree that they shall know that the state is by right theirs, and finally and justly shall come into their own while never relaxing in their efforts to secure the very best economic, social and material improvements in their conditions." This statement by Gompers, before the conservative mold finally jelled, was actually in line with socialist economic theory later developed by Rudolf Hilferding in his *Finanzkapital*. The theory saw the growth of monopoly as inevitable under capitalism. It condemned antimonopoly programs as out of keeping with historical development, and in many instances approved the development of monopoly because such concentration of productive prices would make the transformation to socialism easier. The major concern of the Marxists, therefore, was political. By winning state power they would expropriate the monopolies and take over a fully developed "socialized" mode of production. Only the "social relations" had to be changed. The German unions acquiesced in the cartelization program of German industry, and the English unions early abetted the monopoly devices of British industry. In the United States, however, socialist attention was riveted largely on the trade-agreement policy and Gompers was attacked for "class collaboration." On the monopoly issue in general, the party never defined its stand squarely. In theory and in its arguments with middle-class elements, it prophesied the inevitable concentration of industry. In its politics, however, the party, largely under the influence of agrarian elements in the West, raised political slogans of an antimonopoly nature.

The third dilemma arose out of the limited program of the American Federation of Labor. To the socialists the demand for a shorter work-day and more wages was no solution to the capitalist crisis. Some ultimate goal had to be fixed lest the workers gain illusions that the trade union was a sufficient instrument for melioration. If one accepts the viewpoint that the union, by its own nature, becomes an end in itself and an integral part of capitalist society, then such a socialist theory makes sense. If, however, one regards unionism as a social force which by its own position in an industrial hierarchy becomes a challenge to managerial power and changes the locus of power in capitalism, then Gompers' strategy of focusing on the day-to-day issues was undeniably correct. This is the very problem which unionism, now an established and powerful force in the economy, faces today.

31

Benjamin Stolberg:
The Greatness of Devotion[1]

Benjamin Stolberg, a labor reporter and historian, knew Gompers during his last years. His critique is informed by personal affection joined to a lingering frustration that Gompers, a man of such force and tenacity, could pursue so banal an orthodoxy "resilient only in its safeguards."

For years Samuel Gompers was American Labor. If one traces its victories, one uncovers his tactics. His virtues were the best measure of its social reform. His prejudices, bigoted under stress, became fixed by its trials and errors. Rarely have the native limitations of a leader so perfectly synchronized with the cultural limitations of a movement. Gompers was the clarion consciousness of the unconscious wishes and fears of the tribal period—the primitive craft phase—of American Labor. He was the Moses of its forty years in the wilderness, its daily struggle for manna, its defense against inner rebellion and outer attack.

It is hard to tell Moses from Israel during those forty years in the desert. Guerrilla existence demanded such high-handed leadership of such narrow idealism that the fire of the leader blinds us to the terrible trail behind him. It was only when those simple tribes were brought to the threshold of their greater social significance that his spirit cooled and clarified against the background of their stern epic. His work done, he went to the top of a mountain and died. His death revealed that he was not much of a prophet, for his vision was limited by his watchful pugnacity. He was not much of a thinker, for the same reason. He was a great personal chieftain, whose narrow righteousness was never disturbed by philosophical doubts or utopian dreams.

It is idle to fall into the rhythm of analogy. But the strength of Gompers was of just that kind. He was a personal leader—vigilant,

[1] From Benjamin Stolberg, "What Manner of Man Was Gompers?" *The Atlantic Monthly* 135 (March 1925): 404–12. Reprinted by permission of *The Atlantic Monthly*.

dictatorial, canny, incorruptible, narrow in his ideals though wide in his sympathies. Gompers had the physical spell of the personal leader. When seated, the powerful, long-armed torso and the enormous head seemed to belong to a six-footer. But when he rose his hefty, absurd little legs kept him from soaring above five feet four and gave a touch of anthropoid strength to his chronic restlessness. The head was magnificent. It looked like an animated boulder, on which the weathers of a rich and dangerous life had carved large and rugged yet tremulously sensitive features. The granite complexion, the mossy tufts of graying hair, the Oriental cast of countenance—its whole noble freakishness fascinated. His face was perpetually acute, forever approving or disapproving with the entire gamut of strong emotion. When he felt very intensely his pellucid gray eyes, perched wide apart behind bits of thin windowglass, gave the impression of inflaming his face. The mouth was a wide slit, with the corners quivering down the hard and well-rounded jaw. The voice had the rare and exquisite gift of communicating any emotion he felt. All his vital expressions rose and fell together as though controlled by some inner mechanism. One moment the mobile mask would be cunningly furtive and quizzical, then intimately and wistfully kind; then again it would glow with a self-righteous passion that in retrospect seemed grotesque. It was a congenitally histrionic face, and its outlay in spiritual energy bespoke an enormous vitality.

Physically, and especially nervously, he was tireless. Inhumanly grueling labor and a Gargantuan intemperance seemed to make no impression on him. He had the iron man's disregard for all commonsense in matters of diet, sleep, pleasure, drink, comfort, and work. Years on end his work-day began shortly after eight in the morning and ended deep in the night. Even his relaxations—which he often took in one of the cheap burlesque houses on Pennsylvania Avenue in Washington or in a saloon frequented by the Labor crowd—were spent with some friend or foe in the everlasting game of Labor strategy. His mere animal spirits roused the elementary admiration which we all have for those who are able to go on forever. And even brief contact with his impassioned, prudential, ceaseless alacrity left one fatigued, pleasantly if the relation was pleasant, distempered if otherwise. But even his closest associates rarely left him with a sense of indifference.

His intensity simplified his nature. His tactics, no matter how oblique or vicarious, were intuitional and not intellectual. In his likes and dislikes he was childishly stubborn. And in the women who played a part in his life he called forth mainly the maternal affection. The first Mrs. Gompers, whom he married when he was seventeen and she a bit younger, and with whom he lived in homely comradeship for fifty-four years, mothered his gifts and adjusted herself to his short-comings by overlooking them. She slipped into the rôle of making a home for his cause and it was charming to see the fine friendship which existed between this plain little Jewish housewife and the Scotch-Irish Labor oligarchy which moved around her husband.

For a long generation his personal secretary was Miss Guard. And when toward the end of his life the Bright's disease from which he had suffered for many years affected his heart, Miss Guard nursed him with infinite patience. She would interrupt important conferences to force on him a pill or a spoonful of medicine, much to his peevish disgust, which occasionally precipitated a scene. She knew his every reaction and softened their effects on himself with the shrewdness of friendship, fooling him when he needed or wanted to be fooled and giving him a piece of her mind whenever he needed a censor.

His research secretary was Miss Thorne, who knows as few others the pawns and forces in American Labor. In time she selflessly trained her mind into the shadow of his to such perfection that students of Labor and writers who went to Gompers for his opinions almost always came to her afterward for the real facts and psychology back of them. And she explained and extended his views with rare faith and diplomacy. The devotion with which these two splendid old maids admired, understood, interpreted, and forgave him is remarkable, for there was much in his life and language and ways of doing things which they would have deeply resented in others. The secret probably lay in the fact that to them he was both a great leader and a bad boy.

Unconsciously Gompers surrounded himself with far lesser men. Mr. Matthew Woll, who was derisively called his "crown prince" or "office boy," was and still is the only man of marked ability on the executive council of the Federation. The others drifted to the important positions either through a combination of seniority and conformity or, as Labor people express it, because they are "good poker-players" and play any game accordingly. Gompers invariably held the best hand. They were his creatures, not at all in any invidious, but in the purely malleable, sense. He instinctively picked them because their minds were certain to fade into his. They shared his ideas, which were mediocre, while they lacked his élan, which was his strength. Constitutionally the office of President of the American Federation of Labor is very weak. He can call no strikes; he can settle none. When he issues a call for a boycott it has none but moral force. The Federation is often called a rope of sand. Its treasury is far weaker than the treasuries of most well-sized unions. The office is entirely one of moral authority, of suasion, of tactics and countertactics, of maintaining nice balances through the juggling of forces. Gompers could play this game—sympathetically, ruthlessly, understandingly, cunningly—

with the perfection of a creative artist. Often the leaders were mistrust-
ful of one another, but they could always finally trust him. He had
given himself to the movement completely—and they felt it. He understood them better than they did themselves—and they knew it. He
was the moral centre of their cause. They often strayed to its periphery;
but they never dared to leave the circle of his influence, for beyond
its reach was the camp of the enemy.

He held them together with all the devices of the superb politician.
But fundamentally he kept his machine through the force of morale.

Gompers had the mental characteristics of the personal leader. He
was vastly experienced. The social politics of this country for the last
half-century were his personal reminiscences. One morning he sketched
for me the so-called concerted movement in allied crafts, on which I
had spent a good half-year in research and travel. He told me all I
already knew about it in a brief half-hour, and then he told me some
things about it which no amount of study could have unearthed. He
had gone through the vortex of every political campaign since Gar-
field—in most states of the Union. He had been in the thick of the
fight for or against every bit of social legislation since the late seventies. He carried in his retentive mind the motion picture of the last
half-century of our social history, which alone would have made him
one of the best historians of that period, were it not for the fatal cen-
sorship of his frequently bigoted retrospections and prejudices.

Then he was uncannily shrewd. One by one he outwitted his opponents and rivals, driving them off the confines of the mass movement of American Labor, away to the left and into the desert with
nothing to face but their own embittered Atlantis. He had the fighter's
cold-hot fury, merciless, savagely invective and personal yet superbly
controlled during the struggle; but instantly ready to compromise
when compromise amounted to victory, and completely forgiving the
moment he won. He was above personal grudges, though he was never
so weak as to believe that in politics one can fight ideas without hitting their carriers. These two qualities, his monumental experience
and his sharp skill, welded by his impassioned self-righteousness, gave
the impression of wisdom. He gave such good precedents for his con-
summate strategies that one had the feeling of a synthetic understanding behind them. Great character often gives this illusion. Thus
Gandhi's mystical genius so obscures the naïve nonsense of his beliefs
in a world without laws, medicine, and machinery that his observations seem profound. Gompers had the same necromantic influence, not
merely on himself and his followers, but also on his dissenters. Everybody praised or indicted his social philosophy.

But as a matter of fact that's just what he lacked. He had no long view either of life or of Labor. And the strength as well as the weakness of American Labor under his leadership lay in its hourly realism. When he ventured into philosophical speculations about the State or industrial society he was invariably sophomoric. He had the Jewish admiration for learning, but it was superficial. He read a good deal in the social sciences, but always to prove his own prejudices. And even in his serenest intellectual moments he thought not in search of truth but in terms of debate.

Thus for over forty years he fought the different socialist schools, from the blackest anarchism to the reddest Bolshevism. Yet he admitted to me that he had never studied Marx or Bakunin or Kautsky or Lenin, let alone the historical or theoretical implications of their thought. Of Bolshevism he had this to say: "Bolshevism in Russia began in prohibition. For prohibition uproots the habits of a people" —thus linking his two pet abominations. Of the wars of the pamphlets in which these Red leaders had engaged he knew absolutely nothing. And since the history of European Labor consists so largely of its reactions to the splits in the Social Democracy, he was so woefully ignorant about it as to be a source of perpetual wonder to his European comrades. . . .

. . . Here and there, especially in the needle and railroad industries, they ["New Unionists"] are establishing boards of mutual control and impartial arbitration. And they share contractually in the resulting benefits. In the words of one of their leaders, "organized Labor is passing the stage of mere economic haggling. It is still bargaining. But it is bargaining for a way of life." Now the illuminating thing about Gompers is that he fought this essentially conservative way of life just as hard, though far more covertly, as he fought the radical way of life. And for the same instinctive reason. The New Unionists threatened to lift his bushwhacking opportunism into an industrial programme. They threatened to weaken his jealous craft-separatism, with its absurd "jurisdictional disputes" in the face of the amalgamation of capital. In short, they wanted more peace, while Gompers lived on fighting. He was born to infight at close range: for a little more money —penny by penny; for a little more leisure—minute by minute; for a little more leeway—rule by rule; through the weapon of the strike and the armistice of its 'settlement.' And he hoped to orchestrate the discordant trades in each industry so slowly that no leader might lose his job or his power.

All his life Gompers fought these "intellectuals"—the radicals in the Labor movement, the outside liberals and reformers who were "butting in," the New Unionists. Since the war his anti-intellectualist attitude developed into unreasonable hatred of anybody with a formal training or a liberal education who took an interest in Labor other-

wise than as a hired "expert." This obsession grew on him because he
instinctively felt that the Labor movement *was* outgrowing its primitive craft-phase; that it *was* becoming a way of life; that the forty
years in the wilderness *were* closing; and that his leadership was bound
to wane in time. His own era was really from the early eighties of the
last century until our entry into the war. Since then he felt in himself the struggle between the old and the new. He was too self-righteous
ever to admit even to himself that he might be wrong. But, like all
perfect tacticians, he had an inner censor that warned him when his
opponents expressed genuine unrest in the rank and file. And in the
last few years he inspired several counter-reformations against his
own orthodoxy. When the trades-unions became too fratricidally "autonomous," he manœuvred the progressives in the American Federation of Labor into pressing successfully for the different industrial
"Departments" in the Federation. These Departments are mere clear-
ing-houses for all the trades in one industry. But they appeased the
rank-and-file wish for closer coöperation, and the leaders could be
trusted not to lose their jobs by amalgamating their unions. When
in the last presidential campaign it seemed that the advocates of independent political action were gaining in strength, Gompers "nonparti-
sanly" endorsed La Follette, to whom he was bound by ties of genuine
friendship. Had La Follette won a strong congressional bloc, Gompers
would have won with the winner. As it was, Gompers was able to
smash completely his Socialist and other third-party opponents at the
last national convention of the American Federation of Labor, where
he fought his last fight. But, whether in retreat or attack, he always
fought with the same heads-I-win-tails-you-lose keenness. The detail
of his playing both ends against the middle was a joy to observe. And,
paradoxically, his sincerity was deepest in his very conviction that, as
long as *he* was loading the dice, Labor was safe.

His struggle against capital and the judiciary required much less
acumen. It needed mainly two qualities, morale and industry. And he
had no end of both.

In 1908 he was sentenced to one year in prison for contempt of an
injunction against Labor's boycott of Buck's Stove and Range Company. He never served the sentence. But no one who knew him could
doubt his contemptuous sincerity: "That's all right. Prison holds no
terrors for me. My fare cannot be simpler. My bed cannot be plainer.
And the rest might do me good." His answer to the "injunction
judges" was equally fearless:—

"Only bigoted, power-lusting judges refuse to admit that the abuses
of government by injunction cry to Heaven. They are pure judicial
usurpations without any warrant in law."

The central task of the American Federation of Labor is to organize the unorganized workers, which means chronic warfare against the most conservative section of capital. Under the Gompers régime, since 1882 its membership grew from a scant 50,000 to about 3,000,000. The executive routine of this growth under continuous fire was enormous, and Gompers carried most of its administrative as well as tactical responsibilities. In fact, his intra-Labor quarrels centred largely about this same problem of speed and method in organizing the unskilled workers. We have seen how he resisted the radical demand in the Federation for the spread of class-consciousness. He showed the same stubbornness toward capital. "There is not one word," so he once indirectly addressed a group of employers, "which I have said upon the question of Labor that I would unsay except to say it more emphatically. There is not one step that I have taken which I would retrace except to take it more firmly."

It would be difficult to pass a more critical judgment on his orthodoxy, resilient only in its safeguards.

But Gompers's immediate strength as a leader was his intense humanness. Nothing human ever escaped his sensitive spirit. He was not merely abidingly kind to those who did not cross him. He understood the arts of warmth and affection. His histrionic temper enjoyed being delicately decent, befitting the person and the moment. His pity was instant and unquestioning. His democracy was not ulterior but natural. He recognized sincerity even in his bitterest foes. "Isn't it a pity that such an intelligent fellow as Foster should make such an ass of himself?" he once remarked to me. His zest of life was richly spontaneous and communicative, and his humor, both subtle and spiced, was infectious in his own enjoyment of it.

His friends simply could do no wrong. When they felt like it they could "tell Sam where to get off" with a personal frankness which was amazing. Toward them he dropped all his shrewdness and was absolutely guileless. When he was shown the confession of the McNamara brothers of having dynamited the Los Angeles Times Building, he was dazed by their treachery: "That's terrible. . . . If John McNamara had told me in confidence that he was guilty, I don't believe I would have betrayed him. I am willing to stand by it—I don't believe I would have betrayed him. But I certainly would not have declared my confidence in him. I certainly would not have raised money for his defense." Gompers had fought violence in Labor all his life. Still, McNamara was a Labor man: "I don't believe I would have betrayed him." Clearly Gompers was class-conscious; not in the technical revolutionary sense, but class-conscious none the less. . . .

Gompers could never quite rid himself of the sense of being an immigrant Jew, aggravated by his inevitable malignment as a "Labor agitator." He was far above being either proud or ashamed of his race. For the Jewish faith he had the same strong private dislike he felt for all religion—not merely in form, but in spirit as well. He had the normal man's liking for his own people. At a recent convention he invited the delegates from one of the needle trades, all Jews, to spend an evening with him. "Let's have a little party. I want to be with my own people for a change. I want to get away from these Irish roughnecks," he said, with a slyly affectionate wink at the "roughnecks" present. But he did feel intensely, and justly, that the head of American Labor must be American.

Normally his patriotism was a very fine thing. He loved his country for the sufficient reason that it was his. But during the war, and to some degree after, his alien-Jew-agitator complex may have had something to do with his rather blatant one-hundred-percentism, as some who were close to him felt. Still, there was a good deal of shrewdness mixed with his nationalist frenzy. When the war broke out, he clearly foresaw the wartime legislation in favor of Labor. He saw in the war "the disenthrallment of the American worker of every vestige of wrong and injustice." He felt that then and there was Labor's supreme chance to accelerate its standard of living. And the trend of his mind appears very clearly in the rhetorical question he asked the American people early in 1918 in a public address, and in his own sanguine answer to it: "When the war is over, do you think that . . . Labor will be thrown aside? Not on your life!"

Gompers felt about the "disenthrallment" of Labor much as Lincoln felt about the preservation of the Union. Anything goes!

Such devotion touches greatness. The secret of his strength was in the paradoxically selfless egocentricity with which he harmonized his person and his crusade. He lost his life in his cause and he never troubled to find it. He died at the very end of his era and in the midst of his job.

And such a death was really all he wanted from life.

Afterword

In the 1870s, during the crucial debates over the proper role of trade unions in emerging industrial America, Adolph Strasser rhetorically asked a socialist opponent: "Where are the followers of [Utopian socialist] St. Simon, R[obert] Owen, Fourier, Cabet and Weitling? These people had such an influence on the Labor Movement. [But] they ignored and condemned [the] Trade Unionism emerging from real needs and conditions." [1] At the close of his life in 1924, Gompers, a disciple of Strasser and his "pure and simple" philosophy, might well have asked similar questions: Where are the Utopians, Edward Bellamy and Henry George? What has happened to the T. V. Powderly and the Knights of Labor? Where are the followers of Daniel DeLeon? What happened to the socialist legions of Eugene Debs? Morris Hillquit? Big Bill Haywood and William Z. Foster? What was the fate of the panaceas, free silver and populism? And Gompers' opponents might have replied: Where are the pure and simple ideas of the past? What of the millions of workers never organized by the AFL? Who has triumphed: Gomperism, Capitalism or Radicalism?

There were no clear answers to these many questions then and there appear no definitive answers in our own time. Bellamy, George, free silver and populism are noble curios in the American museum of lost causes. DeLeon's followers still exist and in mixed tribute to the man and his ideas, it may be said that while they never surrendered a sacred principle of the Master, neither did they ever win a strike or affect the condition of man, at least in this world. Foster renounced both his anarchosyndicalist past as well as his AFL organizer role and for forty years was the chief Stalinist spokesman for American communism. Hillquit and the middle of the road socialists were first enthusiastic about, and then disillusioned by, Soviet Russia. The Socialist party continues to run presidential candidates on a quadrennial basis, headed by sweet and innocuous middle-class intellectuals. Radicals never succeeded in capturing the AFL or its successor organizations. The communists, on the other hand, were enormously influential in the 1930s and their heroic organizing abilities led to the establishment of the CIO. Indeed, up to the present, a number of unions, mainly outside of the AFL-CIO, are strongly controlled by communist

[1] Adolph Strasser, *Social-Democrat*, September 24, 1876. Quoted in H. M. Gitelman, "Adolph Strasser and the Origins of Pure and Simple Unionism," *Labor History* 6 (Winter 1965): 78.

leaders who remain in office not through the strength of their ideological persuasion so much as by their forcefulness in pressing employers for pure and simple material gains.

Business opposition to unionism intensified after Gompers died. Company unions, a parody of worker organizations, grew considerably in the 1920s, aided by court decisions which more or less nullified the magna carta of Gompers' dreams, the Clayton Antitrust Act. Union and AFL membership stabilized and then declined in the '20s. The Great Depression and the coming of the New Deal radically changed the organizational, though not the theoretical basis of unionism. The Norris Anti-Injunction and the National Recovery Administration Acts encouraged and then protected union organization. Workers in mass industries—motor, steel, chemical—were brought first into the AFL and then split off into the CIO returning once more in the 1950s to form an imperfect AFL-CIO. The railroad unions, courted in vain by Gompers, never joined a national union complex. But the gains in unionization, even though assisted by friendly national administrations, still met deep and sustained employer opposition. "Although private employers in Western Europe have long taken unions more or less for granted," writes a distinguished economic historian, "the ideology of the workers does not normally return the compliment. In the United States by contrast, it is the right of existence of the union that has been denied, while workers have taken the private employer for granted." [2] After the Second World War, breakdowns in collective bargaining and union-leader corruption led to the passing of two major legislative actions which seriously curbed union power: the Taft-Hartley Act in the 1940s and the Landrum-Griffin Act in the '50s. Today unions are part of the national establishment rarely dealing with ideological questions, mainly concerned with the Gompers heritage of bread-and-butter issues and performing in politics according to his old adage of rewarding friends and punishing enemies. Student rebels who protest anti-Negro union bias or worker support for the Vietnam war provoke anti-intellectual comments from labor leaders remarkably similar to Gompers' speeches of seventy years ago on "effete intellectuals," and "college professor meddlers."

Essentially, then, Gompers was a survivor. The Knights of Labor disappeared, socialist dual unions collapsed, panaceas often proclaimed with enthusiasm died with heartbreak, attempts to form labor parties failed and the Co-Operative Commonwealth never evolved. If union men were asked today, as Gompers was by Hillquit in 1915, "What are your ultimate goals?" their reply would echo his then: they have none. They merely want more—more money, more leisure, more

---

[2] John Kenneth Galbraith, *Economics and the Art of Controversy* (New Brunswick: Rutgers University Press, 1955), p. 11.

security, more freedom from management. Perhaps that was why Gompers refused to radicalize the AFL or follow tactics which led away from pure and simple materialism. When a friend begged him to challenge the political order during the great upheavels of the age, Gompers refused: "Where would you have me lead them? Where they have demonstrated their unwillingness to go?" [3]

[3] Gompers to E. Kurzenknabe, December 5, 1896. Samuel Gompers Letterbooks, AFL-CIO Building, Washington, D. C.

Bibliographical Note

The literature on American labor history is vast, technical, and usually dull. With a few exceptions, this condition is unfortunately true for the study of Samuel Gompers. His autobiography, *Seventy Years of Life and Labor* (New York, 1924) while discursive and arbitrary, is indispensable. Bernard Mandel's *Samuel Gompers* (Yellow Springs, Ohio, 1963) is the standard biography even though it suffers from parochialism and a general hostility to Gompers. Most of Gompers' public statements on leading issues are included in the files of *The American Federationist* (1895–1924); some important positions are set forth in various pamphlets and books published during his lifetime. Among the most significant are: *What Does Labor Want?* (New York, 1893), *Organized Labor, Its Struggles, Its Enemies and Fool Friends* (Washington, D. C., 1904), *Labor and the War* (New York, 1919), *The Workers and the Eight-Hour Day* (Washington, D. C., 1915), *The Voluntary Basis of Trade Unionism* (New York, 1925), and, with W. E. Walling, *Out of Their Own Mouths: A Revelation and Indictment of Sovietism* (New York, 1921). Various interrogations of Gompers are reprinted in *The Double Edge of Labor's Sword* (Chicago, 1914), his debates with the Socialist leader, Morris Hillquit; *Mr. Gompers Under Cross Examination (The Lockwood Commission), Investigating Housing Conditions* (New York, 1922), an antiunion, corrupt practices exposé. *The A.F.L. History, Encyclopedia. and Reference Book* (Washington, D. C., 1919 and 1924) is a badly organized but extremely useful collection of Federation positions taken from annual convention proceedings and edited with a pro-Gompers bias. The Gompers Letter-Books in the AFL-CIO Building in Washington and the more extensive Gompers Collection at the Wisconsin State Historical Society (Madison) are interesting but contain few secrets. Minutes of the AFL Executive Council are still closed but have been seen and used by Philip Taft in his *The A.F. of L. in the Time of Gompers* (New York, 1957), a defense of Gompers and the AFL. Taft has written a broader account in his *Organized Labor in American History* (New York, 1964). A good, though again, narrow, study of Gompers' public statements, is Fred Greenbaum, "The Social Ideas of Samuel Gompers," *Labor History* 7 (Winter 1966): 35–61.

Background for the general history of American labor must begin with John R. Commons and his associates' classic *History of Labour in the United States*, 4 vols. (New York, 1918–35). Joseph G. Rayback *A History of American Labor* (New York, 1966), and Henry Pelling *American Labor* (Chicago, 1960) are excellent one-volume histories, Rayback's the more comprehensive and traditional in its interpretations, Pelling's the more provocative and detached. Philip S. Foner, *History of the Labor Movement in the United States* (New York), is very well researched with special emphasis on radicalism, Negro labor and imperialism. Foner writes from a Marxist–Leninist position which becomes tiresome but excusable for the fascinating material he uncovers. Gerald

N. Grob's *Workers and Utopia* and Norman Ware's *The Labor Movement in the United States* are important studies of the Knights of Labor and the emerging AFL. Grob's book is especially helpful in understanding the historical environment shaping Gompers' thought and contains a fine bibliographical essay. On the Haymarket affair and the role of dynamite Henry David, *The History of the Haymarket Affair* (New York, 1936) and Louis Adamic, *Dynamite* (New York, 1931) are standard accounts but see also Philip Taft and Philip Ross, "American Labor Violence: Its Causes, Character and Outcome," in H. D. Graham and T. R. Gurr, eds., *Violence in America* (Washington, D. C., 1969). Populism and the farmer-labor coalition are discussed in C. M. Destler, *American Radicalism: 1865–1901* (New Haven, 1946), and John Hicks *The Populist Revolt* (Minneapolis, 1931). Marc Karson, *American Labor Unions and Politics* (Carbondale, Ill., 1958), is an important study on the role of the Catholic church and Gompers' relationship to Wilsonian Progressivism. Ray Ginger *The Bending Cross* (Rutgers, N. J., 1949), James Weinstein *The Decline of Socialism in America* (New York, 1967), David Shannon, *The Socialist Party of America* (Chicago, 1967), Howard Quint *The Forging of American Socialism* (Indianapolis, Ind., 1964), and Daniel Bell's essay in D. D. Egbert and S. Persons, eds., *Socialism and American Life* (Princeton, 1952) are important accounts of socialism. John H. M. Laslett's *Labor and the Left, 1885–1924* (New York, 1970) is a fresh and provocative study. Quint and Bell devote much of their work to the labor movement. On the National Civic Federation see Marguerite Green, *The National Civic Federation and the American Labor Movement* (Washington, D. C., 1956) and the revisionist James Weinstein's *The Corporate Ideal in the Liberal State—1900–1918* (Boston, 1968).

Gompers' role in the First World War is studied in Henry Pelling *America and the British Left* (New York, 1957) and Ronald Radosh, *American Labor and Foreign Policy* (New York, 1969). On labor injunctions and the law see F. Frankfurter and N. Greene, *The Labor Injunction* (New York, 1924). Gompers and Negro workers are discussed in J. Jacobson, ed., *The Negro and the American Labor Movement* (New York, 1968). For a general background on patterns of historical discrimination see John Higham, *Strangers in the Land* (New York, 1963). Mark Perlman's *Labor Union Theories in America: Background and Development* (Evanston, Ill., 1958) is helpful.

Index

175

GREAT LIVES OBSERVED

Gerald Emanuel Stearn, *General Editor*

Other volumes in the series:

(*continued on following page*)

(continued from previous page)

Theodore Roosevelt, *edited by Dewey W. Grantham*

Stalin, *edited by T. H. Rigby*

Denmark Vesey: The Slave Conspiracy of 1822,
edited by Robert S. Starobin

Booker T. Washington, *edited by Emma Lou Thornbrough*

George Washington, *edited by Morton Borden*